The Search for Messiah

Mark Eastman, M.D.   Chuck Smith

Co-Published by

Joy Publishing
P.O. Box 9901
Fountain Valley, CA 92708

Box 8000 Costa Mesa CA 92628 (714) 979-0706

The Search for Messiah

Scriptural quotations based on the New King James Version of the Bible, Nelson Publishing, unless otherwise specified. Translational emendations, amplifications and paraphrases are by the author.

Mark Eastman, Chuck Smith
The Search for Messiah
ISBN 0–936728–50–7

PRINTED IN THE UNITED STATES OF AMERICA

2, 3, 4, 5, 6, 7, 8, 9, 10–99, 98, 97, 96

Cover Photo, Horsehead Nebulae by David Malin, Courtesy of the Anglo-Australian Observatory.

Cover Designed by John Shaeffer

In the days of the Second Temple there was a custom to fasten a red-colored strip of wool to the head of a goat which was to be sent away on the Day of Atonement. When this red ribbon became white, it was a sign that God had forgiven Israel's sins.

There is a statement in the Talmud that about "forty years before the Second Temple was destroyed...the red wool did not become white!"[1] The same passage informs us that the gates of the Temple swung open on their own accord! The ancient rabbis believed that these events were indicators that the sins of Israel were no longer being forgiven and the Temple would soon be destroyed![2]

What was the reason for these strange events?

Why was this sign that God gave to the Israelites removed?

Was the Levitical system of atoning for sins through animal sacrifice no longer recognized by God?

Find the answers as we

Search for Messiah!

---

[1]Babylonian Talmud, Yoma chapter 39b.
[2]Adapted from *The Messianic Hope*, Arthur Kac, pg. 227

"You must make your choice. Either this man was and is the Son of God: or else a madman or something worse. You can shut Him up for a fool, you can spit at Him and kill Him as a demon; or you can fall at His feet and call Him Lord and God. But let us not come with any patronizing nonsense about His being a great human teacher. He has not left that open to us. He did not intend to."

C.S. Lewis, *Mere Christianity*

"Brethren, my heart's desire and prayer to God for Israel is that they may be saved."

Paul the Apostle (Romans 10:1)

TABLE OF CONTENTS

DEDICATION

To my loving wife Anna. For her patience and love
during fifteen years of marriage. To my children
Jennifer, Matthew and Kristina, may you walk in
the ways of the LORD all the days of your life.

Mark Eastman

FOREWORD

On rare occasions, a book comes along that will truly change the lives of almost everyone that it touches. This is such a book.

In the Bible there is a presentation that was given on a dozen occasions, by seven different people, which invariably produced unusually effective results, and yet it is rarely given today. It was presenting Jesus as the Messiah *entirely from the Old Testament.*

One of the tragedies of the early church was its diversion down a path of anti-Jewishness. It was tragic for the Jewish people, of course, and it was tragic for the church as well. It blinded the church from much of our Jewish heritage, and denied us numerous scriptural insights which are hidden in the Tanakh (Old Testament).

This book explores many of the treasures which lie hidden in the early rabbinic literature as well as the Tanakh itself, and unveils a trove of treasures and insights as a result. These are treasures for the Jew and the Gentile alike. This book is a gateway of discovery for the pilgrim who is serious about his "Search for Messiah."

The Bible consists of sixty-six books, penned by forty authors over a thousand years. Yet Mark Eastman and Chuck Smith's provocative work dramatically demonstrates that the Scriptures evidence an integrity of design and supernatural engineering in its every detail. The skeptic will be challenged, the traditionalist will be awakened, and the Christian deeply enriched. Prepare yourself for a grand adventure, indeed!

Chuck Missler, Coeur d' Alene, Idaho

ACKNOWLEDGMENTS

I would like to thank Pastor Chuck Smith and Chuck Missler for their tremendous personal examples, their outstanding teaching and for instilling in me an excitement for apologetics and the word of God. Thanks to Angie Nash and Julie Corrigan for typing the manuscript and to Bob Sneidar for your help and expertise. Special thanks to Joe Martin, Lucky Jonker, David Hocking, Scott Richards, Hank Hanegraaff, Nick and Joan La Bruno, Chris Melisko, Luis Santos for reviewing the manuscript. Thanks to Steve Babkow and Bob Rico for your suggestions and to my wife for your support during the preparation of this book.

Finally, thanks to Dr. Ted O'Donnell for the challenge and to the Lord for what He has done and for revealing it to me.

Mark Eastman, M.D.

PROLOGUE

"Do you suppose that I came to give peace on earth?
I tell you, not at all, but rather division. For from now
on five in one house will be divided: three against two,
and two against three. Father will be divided against
son and son against father, mother against daughter
and daughter against mother, mother-in-law against
her daughter-in-law and daughter-in-law against her
mother-in-law."(Luke 12:51-53)
Jesus of Nazareth

There is no doubt about it. Jesus of Nazareth has
created more division than any individual that ever walked
the face of the earth. On the one hand, worshipped by
billions as the Messiah and God in human flesh for nearly
2,000 years. On the other, cursed and rejected by the
majority of the first century religious leaders in Israel. As
he declared, he has certainly created enormous division
within households and even the nations of the world.

As a college student I was told many things about
Jesus. I was told that he was a legend, a lunatic or a
deceiver. Many of you have been told this or have come to
these conclusions as well.

However, there is another possibility-that is, that he is
the Messiah!

Several years after graduating from medical school I was
challenged to examine the claims of Jesus Christ. I had
comfortably explained him away as a legend. However,
when I began to examine his claims in the light of prophecy,
first century Messianic expectations and the secular record
of history, I was astonished at what I found. The historical
evidence for Jesus from secular and rabbinical sources

annihilates the idea that he never existed. Therefore, an examination of his claims seemed in order.

Shortly after beginning my research it became crystal clear why Jesus said he would create division. Not only did he declare that he was the Messiah, he also claimed equality with God and stated that he was *the only way* to salvation. It is claims such as these that create the great division. They are so radical, so unprecedented, that they cause us to take sides. Like many people, I was offended by such claims. However, I realized that there are only three options for this carpenter from Nazareth. He is either a devil (liar), a mad man or he is what he declared–Lord and God, and according to him, the only way to salvation!

The claims of Jesus force us into one of two camps. We either believe his claims or we don't. There is no neutral position. Jesus even said so:

"He who is not with Me is against Me, and he who does not gather with Me scatters abroad." Matthew 12:30

It occurred to me that if Jesus is whom he claimed to be, then making statements such as, *"Do you suppose that I came to give peace on earth? I tell you, not at all, but rather division"*, makes sense. This is because if Jesus is not the Messiah, then making such claims would be a poor way to gain a following. On the other hand, if he is the Messiah, then it would make sense to warn his disciples about the division that his claims would cause and the effect that it would have on their lives. No rational man would use such tactics to get elected prime minister, president or Messiah.

The purpose of this book is to examine the claims of Jesus in the light of ancient rabbinical expectations, Bible prophecy and new discoveries from the Dead Sea Scrolls.

If you are an observant Jew, an atheist or an agnostic, you were probably given this book by a friend or loved one. My plea, my challenge is that you put aside your preconceived biases and read this material with an open mind. Don't be like the man who says, "Don't confuse me with facts, I've made up my mind."

My hope is that the evidence presented here will inspire the believer and stir the skeptic to further study.

Mark Eastman

NOTES

CHAPTER 1

THE HOPE FOR MESSIAH

For 3500 years the Jewish people have awaited the arrival of their anointed redeemer, deliverer and savior–the Messiah. God, speaking through Moses, declared:

> "I will raise up for them a Prophet like you from among their brethren, and will put My words in his mouth, and he shall speak to them all that I command him. And it shall be that whoever will not hear My words, which he speaks in My name, I will require it of him." (Deuteronomy 18:18-19)

This passage declares that the Messiah would come from the midst of the Jewish people, yet he would be a great prophet who would speak the very words of God! The passage goes on to claim that whoever does not heed the word of the prophet, believed by many rabbis to be the Messiah, God will hold him in judgment. [1]

The hope for the Messiah is central to the life of the observant Jewish believer. The prayers of the faithful and the teachings of the rabbis down through the ages have focused on this promise. However, many of the beliefs about the Messiah have changed dramatically over the

---

[1] Fourteenth century rabbi Levi Gershon applied this verse as messianic based on Midrash Thanhuma which points to the Messiah as being greater than Moses. Although the Midrash does not state that this is the Messiah, Rabbi Gershon deduces from the Midrash that the Messiah will be "The Prophet." For a discussion of the messianic application of this passage by the rabbis, See *Messianic Prophecy*, Rachmiel Frydland; 1980.

centuries. Early rabbinical beliefs about the mission, character, origin and destiny of the Messiah (450 B.C.E-400 C.E.)[1,2] were radically different from the beliefs of modern rabbis. Dozens of passages in the Tanakh[3] that the ancient rabbis believed referred to the Messiah are interpreted by modern rabbis as non-Messianic! This includes passages of scripture that were interpreted for thousands of years as Messianic. How can this be? Why have the rabbis changed their position on Messianic prophecy? What was the motivation behind the dramatic change in interpretation?

As we examine the various beliefs of the ancient rabbis we will find that not only are they in stark contrast with contemporary Jewish thought, but the ancient views are in almost perfect agreement with Christian beliefs regarding the character, lineage, birth, mission and destiny of the Messiah.

However, despite this fact, some twentieth century Jewish scholars have accused Christians of fabricating the belief that the Messiah would be the Son of God, born of a virgin and that he would come, suffer and die for the sins of the people and then come again.

Listen to the words of one twentieth century Jewish scholar, Samuel Levine:

---

[1]This is the time period in which "Rabbinical Judaism" began and the Talmud, Mishna and Midrash were written.
[2]B.C.E. means Before Common Era as opposed to the Christian "Before Christ". C.E. means common era.
[3]Tanakh is the name for the Jewish Bible used by Orthodox believers. Tanakh is a contraction for Torah (The law)–Nevi'im (The Prophets)–Kethuvim (The Writings). For the purposes of this book we will use the term Old Testament as a synonym for Tanakh.

"As you know, the Jews were in Israel for around 1000
years before Jesus appeared. They had a definite
concept of what the Messiah would be like–there was a
status quo regarding the nature of the Messiah. The
Christians appeared and introduced an entirely
different picture of what the Messiah would be like
(Son of God, God incarnate, born of a virgin, two
comings, etc). Thus, the Christians changed the status
quo concept of the Messiah, and so the full burden of
proof rests upon them."[1]

In the following pages we will discover what the "full
burden of proof" actually reveals. We will take a trip
through time as we examine the ancient and modern
rabbinical interpretations of Messianic prophecy. The
dramatic change in rabbinical Messianic beliefs can easily be
demonstrated by comparing the writings of the rabbis of the
last 2300 years with modern rabbinical interpretations of
Messianic prophecy. You may be as startled as I was when
you read the views of these ancient rabbis. The ancient
rabbinical views are nearly 180 degrees in opposition to
those of modern rabbis. However, the vast majority of
modern Jews have never been taught the ancient views.

An examination of those ancient writings reveals that
the Messianic "status quo" spoken of by Samuel Levine
never existed. Throughout the history of rabbinical thought
there have always been differing beliefs regarding many
aspects of the Messiah's mission and destiny. These views
are expressed and discussed extensively in the ancient
rabbinical writings. The Messianic beliefs found in the
Talmud and the Midrashim represent the majority opinions
of the various rabbinical academies. As we examine these
views we will see that the Christian beliefs regarding the
birth, character, mission and destiny of the Messiah are in

---

[1] *You Take Jesus, I'll Take God,* Samuel Levine, pg. 12, Hamoroh Press,
1980.

most cases identical to those of the ancient rabbinical ones. Therefore, the ancient rabbinical beliefs were not changed but embraced by the Christians. The burden of proof, therefore, rests on modern rabbinical scholarship to explain their radically different view of the Messiah!

The Skeptic Asks

As an agnostic, scientifically trained physician, I had an ongoing struggle with the paradoxical life and claims of Jesus of Nazareth. During my years in college and medical school I had developed sophisticated set of assumptions, pre-suppositions, beliefs, conjectures, theories, rationalizations and mental gyrations in order to explain away the life, claims and even the existence of Jesus of Nazareth. However, his life and its indelible effect on human history defied my every attempt to explain it away.

On the one hand, Jesus has been worshipped as the Messiah, the Son of God, God in human flesh, by billions of people, including millions of Jews, for more than nineteen centuries. In fact, in the last two centuries, there has been an increasing acceptance of the Messiahship of Jesus by many Jews.[1,2] However, during the last nineteen centuries he has also been rejected, despised and even ridiculed by many, including the majority of the Jewish leadership. In fact, in many Bible-believing Jewish families, conversion to Christianity means the loss of one's

---

[1]Among the many testimonies is that of Dr. Alfred Edersheim, a Jewish Messianic scholar. In his book, *"The Life and Times of Jesus the Messiah,"* he compiled over 456 Old Testament passages which ancient rabbis believed referred to the Messiah. Edersheim was born and raised an Orthodox Jew. However, as an adult, after a careful study of Messianic prophecy he became a believer in the messiahship of Jesus of Nazareth.
[2]According to Ariel Ministries, there are at least 100,000 Jews today who accept the Messiahship of Jesus.

Jewishness. Many families even consider such a conversion the equivalent of death! However, if one becomes an atheist, Buddhist, Muslim or an agnostic, you are still accepted as Jewish with open arms!

What is the reason for this sharp dichotomy?

This paradoxical reaction to Jesus raises many difficult questions. Why is Jesus of Nazareth such a point of contention among the Jewish leadership? Was the acceptance of Jesus by some Jews, including such unlikely converts as priests, rabbis and members of the Sanhedrin, the result of a simple difference in interpretation of Messianic prophecy? Was the rejection of the promised Messiah foreseen by the writers of the Hebrew Bible? Was the acceptance of Jesus by some Jews the result of his bodily resurrection proclaimed by the New Testament records?

These, and other issues concerning Jesus, baffled me. I just couldn't believe that the very people who were waiting for the Messiah would fail to recognize him when he came. After all, the ancient rabbis had a keen knowledge of the Scriptures and the Hebrew language. Most would agree that their knowledge of Hebrew was superior to our current knowledge.[1] Consequently, it seemed illogical that they would reject the very leader that they had awaited and studied about in the Scriptures for over a thousand years.

I wondered whether the biblical passages that the early church fathers believed were Messianic were also believed

---

[1]If anyone doubts this statement then I would challenge you to examine the 1985 Jewish Publication Society translation of the Tanakh. At the bottom of nearly every page are footnotes with the words "meaning uncertain" in reference to hundreds of Hebrew words. Certainly the authors of "those unknown words" knew their meaning or they would not have included them in the Holy Scriptures!

to be Messianic by the ancient rabbis? Did the early
Christians go through the Tanakh and pick scriptures out of
context and apply them to the life and Messianic claims of
Jesus? Or, were these same scriptures also believed to be
Messianic by the rabbis of Jesus' day?

Finally, I wondered whether Jesus of Nazareth was
even an historical figure at all. Was his life a fabrication, a
legend, an "ideal," made up by digging through the passages
believed to be Messianic by the rabbis of the day?

This denial of the historicity of Jesus has been a
common approach used by liberal Bible critics and rabbis
over the centuries to explain away the life of the carpenter
from Nazareth. However, there are some very unsettling
questions created in claiming that Jesus was a non-historical
figure. How do you explain the testimony of the early
church? And why would the Jews and the Romans embark
on an all-out persecution of people who believed in a non-
historical figure? It just didn't fit.

The early Christian church was almost exclusively
Jewish. In the face of relentless persecution, and despite the
warnings of the Jewish leadership, thousands of Jews
became immediate believers in the Messiahship of Jesus of
Nazareth. We know from history that in the first few
centuries of Christianity hundreds of thousands of people
were killed for believing in the Messiahship of Jesus.[1]

Why was a belief in the deity of Jesus so important that
Jewish women were willing to endure even watching their
own children being put to death for refusing to worship
Caesar? Why were thousands of first century Jews and
gentiles willing to be crucified, stoned, beheaded, eaten by
lions, burned at the stake and even fried alive in metal pans

---

[1] See *Foxe's Book of Martyrs*.

for belief in Jesus? Why was he embraced with lifelong devotion and material sacrifice by some Jews and yet rejected and cursed by the majority of the Jewish leadership?

Was Jesus simply the author of a well-devised plot to fulfill prophecy? Or was he "Messianized" by his followers after he died? Was the life of this carpenter from Nazareth the fulfillment of the Messianic mission and destiny the rabbis of Jesus' time were expecting? Or was his life the tragic ending of a lunatic, or worse yet, a charlatan? These are some of the questions I set out to answer.

If you are an atheist, an agnostic or an observant Jew, I'd be willing to bet that you have also struggled with the claims of Jesus of Nazareth and the phenomenal impact that this one man has had on planet earth. If he was truly an historical figure then we must explain this impact. He is simply too controversial to ignore.

In my quest to fairly evaluate the claims of Jesus I decided to sift through the evidence of secular history, the sacred Jewish scriptures and the writings of the ancient rabbis to gain an accurate picture of the expected Messiah. I then compared my findings with the life and teaching of Jesus of Nazareth. The result was a stunning "new view" of the life, character, mission and destiny of the Messiah.

Sadly, most Jewish people are now taught a slanted and biased view of Messiah which either ignores or flatly denies the overwhelming consensus of the early Jewish scholars. Our hope is that the evidence presented here will result in a more balanced and accurate understanding of the centerpiece of Jewish hope–the Messiah.

The Hope for Messiah

The hope for the Messiah actually predates the promise recorded by Moses in Deuteronomy chapter 18. For thousands of years the rabbis have recognized that the promise of a redeemer for mankind goes all the way back to the Garden of Eden and is thereafter woven throughout the Tanakh, even up to the last prophet Malachi. The promise of Messiah is so prominent in the biblical text that it led one Talmudic writer to state,

> "All the prophets prophesied only of the days of the Messiah." Babylonian Talmud, Sanhedrin 99a

In Genesis 3:15 we find the promise of a redeemer for mankind given to Adam and Eve after their temptation and fall into sin. After the sin of Adam and Eve we read that God placed a curse on Satan and promised that the *"seed"* of the woman would ultimately bruise the head of the serpent (i.e. Satan).

> "So the LORD God said to the serpent: 'Because you have done this, you are cursed more than all cattle, and more than every beast of the field; on your belly you shall go, and you shall eat dust all the days of your life. And I will put enmity between you and the woman, and between your seed and her Seed; He shall bruise your head, and you shall bruise His heel.'" (Genesis 3:14-15)

In this passage we see the beginning of the spiritual battle between good and evil on planet earth, between the seed of the woman and Satan's seed, culminating in the ultimate conflict between the Messiah and Satan. The ancient rabbis clearly understood that this battle was between the Messiah, the seed of the woman and the usurper Satan.

In the ancient commentary on Genesis 3:15, the Targum Jerusalem states:

> "And it shall be that when the sons of the woman study the Torah diligently and obey its injunctions, they will direct themselves to smite you (Satan) on the head and slay you; but when the sons of the woman forsake the commandments of the Torah and do not obey its injunctions, you will direct yourself to bite them on the heel and afflict them. However, there will be a remedy for the sons of the woman, but for you, serpent, there will be no remedy. They shall make peace with one another in the end, in the very end of days, in the days of the King Messiah"[1,2]

In this Targum we see that the prophecy in Genesis 3:15 was believed to be a reference to the Messiah and his people who diligently follow the Torah. According to this passage it would be the Messiah who would provide the "remedy" for mankind. That is, he was to provide the remedy for man's sin. He would reconcile man back to his Creator. As we will see, even before the very first sin in the Garden of Eden, God's plan of salvation would involve the redemptive work of the Messiah. Anyone who reads the Talmud, or any ancient rabbinical literature, will see the Messiah referred to as "The Holy One of Israel", "The Redeemer of Israel", "The Righteous One" and many other exalted titles. In these references of the Messiah there is the emphasis on his character (being pure from sin), and on the

---

[1]The Targums are Aramaic commentaries on the Tanakh, compiled between 200 B.C.E and 200 C.E.
[2]*The Messiah: An Aramaic Interpretation; The Messianic Exegesis of the Targum*, Samson H , Levy (Cincinnati: Hebrew Union College Jewish Institute of Religion, 1974), pg. 2.

work of redemption that would be accomplished through
his life. As we look further at the mission and work of the
Messiah it will become apparent that his major mission, his
major accomplishment was to be the reconciliation of
mankind back to his Creator.

The Hope During the Talmudic Period

"The World was not Created but only for the
Messiah." Babylonian Talmud, Sanhedrin 98b

The Tanakh (or Old Testament) written in Hebrew and
Aramaic was gradually compiled between about 1450-450
B.C.E. By the year 285 B.C.E., the Jewish canon of
scripture was completed and was being translated into the
common language of Greek. The biblical text we have today
has been proven by textual discoveries to be nearly identical
to the canon of scripture translated in 285 B.C.E.·

After the return of the Jews to Israel, following the
Babylonian captivity, rabbis (teachers) began to compile
commentaries on the entire Hebrew Bible. These
interpretations of scripture were at first transmitted orally,
but by the time of the second century C.E. they were being
compiled in the Mishna, the Talmud, Targumim and
Midrashim in written form. These ancient commentaries
covered nearly all aspects of Jewish law, traditions and
many social issues. (e.g. marriage, divorce, land use, etc.).
However, most importantly, they go into great detail
regarding the Messiah's origin, mission and destiny.

The above quote from the Babylonian Talmud,
Sanhedrin 98b summarizes the exalted view of the Messiah
in the eyes of the rabbis during the Talmudic period, 200
B.C.E.-500C.E. The Mishna, Targums, Talmud and the

Midrashim[1] present a very high view of the Messiah. It is fair to say that the Messiah is the central focus of these incredibly voluminous works written by the ancient rabbis. Every aspect of the origin, life, mission, time of his coming and destiny are discussed in these writings.

The promise of the Messiah is so central to the Bible that, according to the rabbis, prophecies of his mission and destiny are woven both visibly and invisibly throughout the biblical text. The rabbis see two types of Messianic prophecies in the Bible. There were those prophecies that were predictions of some aspect of his life, e.g. birth, lineage, character, mission and destiny. Then there were "types," "shadows" or "similitudes" which were veiled prophecies of some aspect of the Messiah's life.

Alfred Edersheim, the renowned nineteenth century Messianic scholar, states:

> "That a careful perusal of [the rabbinical] scriptural quotations shows that...such doctrines as the pre-mundane existence of the Messiah; his elevation above Moses and even the angels; his representative character; his cruel sufferings and derision; his violent death, and that for his people; his work on behalf of the living and the dead; his redemption, and restoration of Israel; the opposition of the gentiles; their partial judgment and conversion; the prevalence of his law; the universal blessings of the latter days; and his (the Messiah's) Kingdom—can all be clearly be deduced from the unquestioned passages in the ancient rabbinical writings."[2,3]

---

[1] A discussion of these writings can be found in Appendix I.

[2] That is the existence of the Messiah even before the creation of the universe.

[3] *The Life and Times of Jesus the Messiah*, Alfred Edersheim, MacDonald Publishing Co. 1883,pg 164-165.

Therefore, according to Edersheim the ancient rabbinical beliefs on virtually every aspect of the Messiah can be found in their writings. It is those writings that we will draw upon as we try to build the Messianic picture.

In the Talmud, the Messiah was viewed as much more than just a man, much more than a prophet. The term "Messiah" (pronounced "Mashiyach" in Hebrew) means "Anointed One." Although there were many "anointed" priests, kings and prophets in the history of Israel, there was only one Mashiyach–"the Messiah." As we shall see, there is evidence from ancient Hebrew Scriptures that the Messiah would not only be a prophet and redeemer but, *God in human flesh* as well. It is these ancient writings that we will rely upon as we search for the Messiah.

As we examine the writings of the ancient rabbis and the Messianic portrait painted by the Tanakh, we will endeavor to discover whether Jesus of Nazareth or anyone else in history has fulfilled the Messianic composite they were expecting.

CHAPTER 2

THE SUFFERING SERVANT

Throughout the Hebrew Bible there are passages about a righteous servant who would suffer physical abuse, mockery, derision, rejection and finally death. This suffering servant, though pure from sin himself, is wounded because of the sins of the people and through suffering and death, the people of God would be healed.[1] The identity of this suffering servant is, however, a serious point of controversy between Christian and Jewish scholars.

From the first days of the church, Christians have claimed that the suffering servant passages were references to the Messiah and that the rejection, suffering and death of Jesus of Nazareth were evidences for his Messiahship. Peter the Apostle points to the suffering and death of Jesus as a God-ordained plan rather than an unforeseen consequence of a failed ministry:

> "For to this you were called, because Christ also suffered for us, leaving us an example, that you should follow His steps: Who committed no sin, nor was guile found in His mouth, who, when He was reviled, did not revile in return; when He suffered, He did not threaten, but committed Himself to Him who judges righteously, who Himself bore our sins in His own body on the tree, that we, having died to sins, might live for righteousness; by whose stripes you were healed." (1 Peter 2:21-24)

---

[1] Isaiah 52:13-53:12.

13

Here Peter paraphrases Isaiah 53, one of the most famous of the suffering servant passages and declares its fulfillment in Jesus Christ.

Many Old Testament prophecies of a suffering, rejected individual are quoted in the New Testament as Messianic and fulfilled in the life of Jesus. The New Testament records that after his resurrection Jesus even declared that the Messiah must suffer:

> "Then He said to them, 'O foolish ones, and slow of heart to believe in all that the prophets have spoken! Ought not the Christ to have suffered these things and to enter into His glory?' And beginning at Moses and all the Prophets, he expounded to them in all the Scriptures the things concerning Himself." (Luke 24:25-27)

Modern rabbis contend that the suffering servant is not the Messiah. Rather, they claim, he is either an unknown Temple Priest, perhaps King Hezekiah,[1] or even the nation of Israel itself.

Again, twentieth century Jewish author Samuel Levine writes regarding the suffering servant in Isaiah 53:

> "Many Jewish commentators feel that it [Isaiah 53] refers to the Jewish people on the whole. We find many instances in the Bible where the Jewish people on the whole are addressed to, or are described, in the singular....Thus, Isaiah 53 could very well be describing the history of the Jewish people–despised by the world, persecuted by the crusaders and the Spanish Inquisition and the Nazis, while the world silently

---

[1] Babylonian Talmud, Sanhedrin 98a-99b.

watched...The verses therefore do not point exclusively to Jesus, or to a Messiah."[1]

However popular this belief has become in modern Jewish scholarship, it has not been held throughout the history of rabbinical thought. There is abundant written evidence, from ancient rabbinical sources, that the suffering servant is indeed the Messiah.[2] In fact, by the time of the writing of the Mishna and the Talmud, the paradoxical destiny of the Messiah had created a struggle in the minds of the rabbis. In addition to the suffering servant prophecies, the Bible had woven throughout its text the prophecies of a triumphant, ruling and reigning king who would bring everlasting righteousness to the earth and restore Israel to its place of prominence among the nations. This contradiction was too much for the rabbis to unite into one person. So, they began to speculate that there were to be two or possibly three Messiahs!

According to their speculations, the suffering servant, called Messiah Ben Joseph, would be killed in the war of Gog and Magog. The triumphant, ruling and reigning servant, called Messiah Ben David, would rebuild the temple and rule and reign in Jerusalem. This belief eventually became firmly rooted in the Talmud.[3]

There is great disagreement between Jewish and Christian scholars as to whether the suffering servant passages are indeed Messianic. From the Jewish perspective scholars argue, "If any people should have recognized the Messiah, the one who was the focus of their national existence, wouldn't it have been the Jews?" From the Christian perspective, others respond, "But how could

---

[1] *You Take Jesus, I'll Take God*, Samuel Levine, pg. 24-25 Hamoroh Press.1980.
[2] See Appendix IV, Rabbinical Quotes on Isaiah 53.
[3] *The Life and Times of Jesus the Messiah*, Alfred Edersheim, Appendix IX.

God have made the birth, lineage, character, mission and destiny of the Messiah any more obvious?"

Let's look at some of the suffering servant passages from the Hebrew Bible and their ancient interpretations to find the true identity of the one called the "suffering servant."

The Suffering Servant Songs

In the book of Isaiah there are a group of passages called "The Suffering Servant Songs." These four vignettes are found in Isaiah 42:1-7; Isaiah 49:1-6; Isaiah 50:4-9; Isaiah 52:13–53:12. We will focus on the fourth suffering servant song since it is the most disputed portion of Isaiah. [1]

"Behold, My Servant shall deal prudently, He shall be exalted and extolled and be very high. Just as many were astonished at you, so His visage was marred more than any man, and His form more than the sons of men; So shall He sprinkle many nations. Kings shall shut their mouths at Him; for what had not been told them they shall see, and what they had not heard they shall consider. Who has believed our report? And to whom has the arm of the LORD been revealed? For He shall grow up before Him as a tender plant, and as a root out of dry ground. He has no form or comeliness; and when we see Him, there is no beauty that we should desire Him. He is despised and rejected by men, a man of sorrows and acquainted with grief. And we hid, as it were, our faces from Him; He was despised, and we did not esteem him. Surely He has borne our griefs and carried our sorrows; yet we esteemed Him stricken, smitten by God, and afflicted. But He was wounded for our transgressions, He was bruised for our iniquities; the chastisement for our peace was upon

---

[1]Messianically applied in Targum of Jonathan,written between first and second century C.E.

Him, and by His stripes we are healed. All we like
sheep have gone astray; we have turned, every one, to
his own way; and the LORD has laid on him the
iniquity of us all. He was oppressed and he was
afflicted, yet he opened not his mouth; he was led as a
lamb to the slaughter, and as a sheep before its
shearers is silent, so he opened not his mouth. He was
taken from prison and from judgment, and who will
declare his generation? For he was cut off from the
land of the living; for the transgressions of My people
he was stricken. And they made his grave with the
wicked; but with the rich at his death, because he had
done no violence, nor was any deceit in his mouth.
Yet it pleased the LORD to bruise him; he has put him
to grief. When You make his soul an offering for sin,
he shall see his seed, he shall prolong his days, and the
pleasure of the LORD shall prosper in his hand. He
shall see the travail of his soul, and be satisfied. By his
knowledge My righteous servant shall justify many,
for he shall bear their iniquities. Therefore, I will
divide him a portion with the great, and he shall divide
the spoil with the strong, because he poured out his
soul unto death, and he was numbered with the
transgressors, and he bore the sin of many, and made
intercession for the transgressors."

From the time of the development of the written
Talmud (200–500 C.E.) this portion of scripture was
believed to be Messianic. In fact, it was not until the
eleventh century C.E. that it was seriously proposed
otherwise. At that time Rabbi Rashi began to interpret the
suffering servant in these passages as reference to the nation
of Israel.[1]

One of the oldest translations of the Hebrew scriptures
is known as the Targums. These are Aramaic translations of
very ancient Hebrew manuscripts that also included
commentary on the scriptures. They were translated in the

---

[1] See *The Messianic Hope*, Arthur Kac.

first or second century B.C.E. In the Targum of Isaiah, we read this incredible quote regarding the suffering servant in Isaiah 53:

"Behold, My servant **the Messiah** shall prosper; he shall be exalted and great and very powerful. The Righteous One shall grow up before him, lo, like sprouting plants; and like a tree that sends its roots by the water-courses, so shall the exploits of the holy one multiply in the land which was desperate for him. His appearance shall not be a profane appearance, nor shall the awe of an ignorant person, but his countenance shall radiate with holiness, so that all who see him shall become wise through him. All of us were scattered like sheep... **but it is the will of God to pardon** the sins of all of us on his account...Then I will apportion unto him the spoil of great nations...**because he was ready to suffer martyrdom** that the rebellious he might subjugate to the Torah. And he might seek pardon for the sins of many." [1]

According to this commentary, the Messiah would suffer martyrdom, he would be, "The Righteous One" and would provide a way for God to forgive our sins. This forgiveness would be accomplished, not because of our goodness, but on account of the righteousness of Messiah. As we shall see, this is the very message of Jesus as recorded in the New Testament!

A reading from a Yom Kippur and Rosh Hashanah prayer book contains this passage:

"Our righteous anointed is departed from us: horror has seized us, and we have none to justify us. He has borne the yoke of our iniquities, and our transgression, and is wounded because of our transgression. He bears our sins on his shoulders, that we may find pardon for

---

[1] See comments on Isaiah 53 in Edersheim, *The Life and Times of Jesus the Messiah*, Appendix IX.

our iniquities. We shall be healed by his wound, at the time that the eternal will create the Messiah as a new creature. O bring him up from the circle of the earth. Raise him up from Seir, to assemble us the second time on mount Lebanon, by the hand of Yinon." [1,2]

In this beautiful prayer, a commentary on Isaiah 53, we discover several of the ancient beliefs on the mission of God's righteous Messiah:

1) He would apparently depart after an initial appearance: "Our righteous anointed is departed."

2) The Messiah would be the one who justifies the people:[3]

"Horror has seized us, and we have none to justify us."

3) The Messiah would be wounded because of our transgressions and would take upon himself the yoke or punishment of our iniquities.[4]

"He has borne the yoke of our iniquities, and our transgression, and is wounded because of our transgression."

4) By his wound we would be healed when he reappears as a "new creature."

"We shall be healed by his wound, at the time that the eternal will create the Messiah as a new creature."

---

[1] Yinon is one of the ancient rabbinical names of the Messiah.
[2] See *The Messianic Hope*, Arthur Kac, The Chapter of the Suffering Servant.
[3] To justify is to make one acceptable and righteous in the sight of God.
[4] i.e. Our individual sins.

In the Babylonian Talmud there are a number of commentaries on the suffering servant in Isaiah 53. In a discussion of the suffering inflicted upon this servant we find the following statement:

"This teaches us that **God will burden the Messiah** with commandments and sufferings as with millstones."[1]

In another chapter of Sanhedrin we find a discussion on the name of the Messiah. In this remarkable portion of the Talmud we read:

"There is a whole discussion in the Talmud about Messiah's name. The several discussants suggested various names and cited scriptural references in support of these names. The disciples of the school of Rabbi Yehuda Ha' Nasi said 'The sick one is his name,' for it is written, **'Surely he has borne our sicknesses and carried our sorrows and pains, yet we considered him stricken, smitten, and afflicted of God.'**"[2]

In the Midrash we again find reference to the "Suffering Servant" of Isaiah 53. In characteristic fashion we read one rabbi quoting another in a discussion of the Messiah's suffering:

"Rabbi Huna in the name of Rabbi Acha says: 'The sufferings are divided into three parts: one for David and the fathers, one for our own generation, and one for **the King Messiah**, and this is what is written, **'He was wounded for our transgressions.'**"[3]

---

[1]Talmud, Sanhedrin 93b .
[2]Talmud, Sanhedrin 98b.
[3] *The Life and Times of Jesus the Messiah*, Alfred Edersheim, Appendix IX.

In a portion of the Midrash, called the Haggadah (a portion which expounds on the non-legal parts of Scripture) in the tractate Pesiqta Rabbati[1] we read an interesting discussion of the suffering of the Messiah:

> "And the Holy One made an agreement with the Messiah and said to him, '**The sins of those which are forgiven for your sake will cause you to be put under an iron yoke**, and they will make you like this calf whose eyes are dim, and they will choke your spirit under the yoke, and on account of their sins **your tongue shall cleave to your mouth**. Are you willing to do this?' Said Messiah before the Holy One: 'Perhaps this agony will last many years?' And the Holy One said to him: 'By your life and by the life of my head, one week only have I decreed for you; but if your soul is grieved I shall destroy them even now.' But the Messiah said to him: 'Sovereign of the world, with the gladness of my soul and the joy of my heart I take it upon me, on condition that not one of Israel shall perish, and not only those alone should be saved who are in my days, but also those who are hid in the dust; and not only should the dead of my own time be saved, but all the dead from the first man until now; also, the unborn and those whom thou hast intended to create. Thus I agree, and on this condition I will take it upon myself.' " (Pesiqta Rabbati. chapter 36)

Another section of chapter 37, Pesiqta Rabbati, says the following:

> "The Patriarchs will one day rise again in the month of Nisan and will say to the Messiah: '**Ephraim, our righteous Messiah**, although we are your ancestors, you are nevertheless greater than we, **for you have borne the sins of our children**, as it is written: '**Surely he has borne our diseases and carried our sorrows; yet we regarded him stricken,**

---

[1] Compiled in the ninth century, but based on writings from Talmudic times from 200 B.C.E.- 400 C.E.

smitten of God, and afflicted. But he was wounded for our sins, bruised for our iniquities, upon him was the chastisement that makes us well, and through his wounds we are healed.'[1] Heavy oppressions have been imposed upon you, as it is written: '**As a result of oppression and judgment he was taken away**[2]; but in his day, who considered that **he was torn from the land of the living because of the transgressions of my people?**' You have been a laughing stock and a derision among the peoples of the world, and because of you they jeered at Israel, as it is written, You have dwelt in darkness and in gloominess, and your eyes have not seen light, **your skin was cleaving to your bones, and your body withered like wood.** Your eyes became hollow from fasting, and **your strength was dried-up like a potsherd,** as it is written.[3]All this happened because of the sins of our children, as it is written: 'And Jehovah laid on him the iniquities of us all.' " (Isaiah 53:6)

In these fascinating portions of the Midrash we see language which closely parallels Psalm 22.[4] The writer specifically ties together the sufferings of the pierced servant in Psalm 22 (tongue shall cleave to your mouth…dried up like a potsherd) with the servant in Isaiah 53, whose sufferings provide a way for the children of Israel to be saved. The fact that the writer of this portion of the Midrash would tie the sufferings of the servant in Psalm 22 (the pierced one) and Isaiah 53, the despised and rejected one, is nothing less than astonishing. Clearly at least some of the rabbis of the ancient Midrashim believed that the Messiah would suffer and that the sufferings found in Psalm 22 and Isaiah 53 belong to the same person.

---

[1] A reference to Isaiah 53.
[2] A reference to the death of the Messiah.
[3]A reference to Psalm 22:15-16.
[4]In fact, there is no other portion of scripture that parallels the language in Pesiqta Rabbati chapter 37 as closely as does Psalm 22.

In the eleventh century C.E. the rabbinical interpretation of Isaiah 52-53 began to change. Rabbi Rashi, a well-respected member of the Midrashim, began to interpret this portion of scripture as a reference to the sufferings of the nation of Israel. However, even after this interpretation took root, there remained many dissenters who still held onto its original, Messianic view.

In the fourteenth century Rabbi Moshe Cohen Crispin, a strong adherent to the ancient opinion, stated that applying the suffering servant of Isaiah 53 to the nation of Israel :

"distort[s] the verses of their natural meaning…As then it seemed to me that the doors of the literal interpretation [of Isaiah 53] were shut in their face, and that 'they wearied themselves to find the entrance', **having forsaken the knowledge of our Teachers, and inclined after the 'stubbornness of their own hearts' and of their own opinion, I am pleased to interpret it, in accordance with the teaching of our Rabbis, of the King Messiah,** and will be careful, so far as I am able, to adhere to the literal sense: thus possibly, I shall be free from the forced and farfetched interpretations of which others have been guilty. This **prophecy was delivered by Isaiah at the divine command for the purpose of making known to us something about the nature of the future Messiah, who is to come and to deliver Israel,"** [1]

Rabbi Isaac Abrabanel (1437-1508), a member of the Midrashim, made the following remarkable declaration regarding the suffering servant of Isaiah 53:

---

[1] A Commentary of Rabbi Mosheh Kohen Ibn Crispin of Cordova. For a detailed discussion of this reference see *The Fifty Third Chapter of Isaiah According to Jewish Interpreters*, preface pg. x, S.R. Driver, A.D. Neubauer, KTAV Publishing House, Inc., New York, 1969.

"The first question is to ascertain to whom this
prophecy refers, for the learned among the Nazarenes
expound it of the man who was crucified in Jerusalem
at the end of the Second Temple, and, who according
to them, was the Son of God and took flesh in the
virgin's womb, as is stated in their writings. **Jonathan
ben Uzziel interprets it in the Targum of the
future Messiah; and this is also the opinion of
our learned men in the majority of their
Midrashim.**"[1]

Two centuries later we find the comments of another
member of the Midrashim, Rabbi Elijah De Vidas, a
Cabalistic scholar in sixteenth century. In his comments of
Isaiah 53 we read:

"The meaning of '**He was wounded for our
transgressions, bruised for our iniquities,**' is,
that since **the Messiah bears our iniquities,
which produce the effect of his being bruised**, it
follows that **who so will not admit that the
Messiah thus suffers for our iniquities must
endure and suffer them for himself.**"[2]

We have also the writings of the sixteenth century
Rabbi Moshe el Sheikh, who declares in his work
"Commentaries of the Earlier Prophets," regarding the
suffering servant in Isaiah 53:

"Our rabbis with one voice accept and affirm the
opinion that **the prophet is speaking of the King
Messiah, and we shall ourselves also adhere to
the same view.**" [3]

---

[1]"*The Messianic Hope*", by Arthur Kac, pg. 75.
[2]ibid, pg. 76.
[3]ibid, pg. 76.

These remarkable references from the ancient rabbis leave no doubt that the suffering servant in Isaiah 52:13– 53:12 was indeed believed to be the Messiah. Even more remarkable is the fact that the suffering servant of Isaiah is connected with the suffering servant of Psalm 22. Finally, we find the ancient rabbis claiming that the suffering and death of the Messiah would have the effect of freeing us from our sins. This is in complete agreement with the Christian concept of the Messiah!

Even without these ancient references, there are several other reasons why the suffering servant in Isaiah 53 could not be the nation of Israel.

First, the suffering servant is an innocent person without sin:

"And they made his grave with the wicked; but with the rich at his death, because he had done no violence, nor was any deceit in his mouth." Isaiah 53:9

Israel has an admittedly sinful past; the Hebrew scriptures even admit this fact. Psalm 14:2-3 says:

"There is none that does good, no not one."

I Kings 8:46 says:

"...for there is no one who does not sin."

Ecclesiastes 7:20 says:

"For there is not a just man on earth who does good and does not sin."

Secondly, the suffering servant of Isaiah 53 suffers on account of the sins of others.

"Surely he has borne our griefs and carried our sorrows; yet we esteemed him stricken, smitten by God, and afflicted. But he was wounded for our transgressions, he was bruised for our iniquities; the chastisement of our peace was upon him, and by his stripes we are healed. All we like sheep have gone astray; we have turned, every one, to his own way; and the LORD has laid on him the iniquity of us all." (Isaiah 53:4)

Thirdly, the suffering servant of Isaiah 53 is willing to suffer.

"He was oppressed and he was afflicted, yet he opened not his mouth; he was led as a lamb to the slaughter, and as a sheep before its shearers is silent, so he opened not his mouth." (Isaiah 53:7)

In the entire history of their nation, the Jews have never suffered willingly.

Finally, the suffering servant's end was death.

"Therefore I will divide him a portion with the great, and he shall divide the spoil with the strong, because **he poured out his soul unto death**, and he was numbered with the transgressors, and he bore the sin of many, and made intercession for the transgressors." (Isaiah 53:12)

The nation of Israel has suffered much, but she has never died. In fact, the nation of Israel was re-gathered back into the land after nearly 1900 years of world-wide dispersion, an event unprecedented in world history.

"Let Israel now say; Many a time they have afflicted me from my youth; Yet they have not prevailed against me." (Psalm 129:1)

Finally, listen to the words of nineteenth century
Jewish scholar Herz Homberg;

"This prophecy is disconnected with what precedes it.
According to the opinion of Rashi and Ibn Ezra, it
relates to Israel at the end of their captivity; the term
'servant' and the use of the singular number referring
to the individual members of the nation. But if so,
what can be the meaning of the passage, '**He was
wounded for our transgressions?**', etc.? Who was
'**wounded?**' Who are the '**transgressors**' Who
'**carried**' the sickness and '**bare**' the pains? And
where are the sick? **Are they not the same as those
who are 'smitten' and who 'bear?**' And if 'each
turned to his own way', upon **whom did 'the Lord
lay the iniquity of them all?**' The Ga'on, Rabbi
Sa'adyah, explains the whole Parashah of Jeremiah:
and there are indeed numerous parts of Scripture in
which we can trace a great resemblance to what befell
Jeremiah while persecuted by the false prophets. But
the commencement of the prophecy, '**He shall be
high and exalted and lofty exceedingly**', and
similarly the words '**with the mighty he shall
divide the spoil**', will not admit of being applied to
him. The fact is that it refers to the King Messiah,
who will come in the latter days, when it will be the
Lord's good pleasure to redeem Israel from among the
different nations of the earth...**and even the
Israelites themselves will only regard him as
'one of the vain fellows', believing none of the
announcements which will be made by him in
God's name**, but being contumacious against him,
and averring that all the reproaches and persecutions
which fall to his lot are sent from heaven, for that he
is '**smitten of God**' for his own sin. For they will not
at first perceive that whatever he underwent was in
consequence of their own transgression, **the Lord
having chosen him to be a trespass-offering**, like
the scapegoat which bore all the iniquities of the house
of Israel. Being, however, himself aware that **through
his pains and revilings the promised redemption
will eventually come** at the appointed time, he will

endure with a willing soul, neither complaining nor
opening his mouth in the siege and distress wherewith
the enemies of Israel will oppress him (as is pointed
out from the passage here in the Haggadah)."[1]

Here we have in the clearest term possible the belief
that the prophet was speaking of King Messiah.
Furthermore, Homberg states that the Messiah, when he
comes, will be rejected "as *one of the vain fellows,
believing none of the announcements which will be made
by him in God's name.*" Finally, he sees the rejection and
death of the Messiah accomplishing the role of the
trespass-offering for the sins of the people. The Messiah
suffers not because of the sins of himself, but on account of
the sins of the people. Through Messiah's suffering and
death *"the promised redemption will eventually come!"*

As we will see, in his understanding of Isaiah 53,
Herzog has pointed out the very heart of the Christian
message!

Psalm 22 "The Pierced One"

One of the most graphic and controversial portions of
scripture is Psalm 22. The passage is disputed because of
the nature of the sufferings it describes and because of the
two different interpretations applied by Christian and
Jewish Bible scholars. As we have already seen in the above
discussion, the rabbis of the ancient Midrashim tied the
sufferings of the Messiah figure in Isaiah 53 to those of the
suffering servant of Psalm 22. However, today most
modern rabbis deny the Messianic application of Psalm 22.

---

[1]From the exposition of the entire Old Testament, called Korem, by Herz
Homberg (Wein, 1818).

"My God, my God, why have You forsaken me? Why are You so far from helping me, and from the words of my groaning?... They cried to You, and were delivered; They trusted in You, and were not ashamed. But I am a worm, and no man; A reproach of men, and despised of the people. All those who see me laugh me to scorn; They shoot out the lip, they shake the head, saying, he trusted in the LORD, let him rescue him; Let him deliver him, since he delights in him! Many bulls have surrounded me; Strong bulls of Bashan have encircled me. They gape at me with their mouths, as a raging and roaring lion. I am poured out like water, And all my bones are out of joint; my heart is like wax; It has melted within me. My strength is dried up like a potsherd, And my tongue clings to my jaws; You have brought me to the dust of death. For dogs have surrounded me; The assembly of the wicked has enclosed me. They pierced my hands and my feet; I can count all my bones. They look and stare at me. They divide my garments among them, and for my clothing they cast lots...For he has not despised nor abhorred the affliction of the afflicted; Nor has he hidden his face from him; But when he cried to him, he heard...All the ends of the world shall remember and turn to the LORD, and all the families of the nations shall worship before You...They will come and declare his righteousness to a people who will be born, that he has done this." (Psalm 22:1, 5-8, 12-18, 24, 27, 31)

In these verses we find the rejection, mocking and death of a righteous servant of God, one "who trusted in the Lord" from the time of his birth, and did not despise the affliction he endured. Yet this Righteous One was a reproach to the people, a "worm," "scorned,"one whose hands and feet were pierced and one so overcome with thirst that his tongue cleaved to his mouth.

The identity of this suffering servant is, to say the least, a point of great contention. The description of his physical suffering bears a striking resemblance to crucifixion, including the bleeding ("poured out like water"), the dehydration ("tongue cleaves to my mouth") and the disarticulation (dislocation of the joints) that occurs in crucifixion ("all my bones are out of joint"). Of course, Christians claim that this is a prophecy of the crucifixion of the Messiah, Jesus of Nazareth.

Perhaps the most controversial portion of the scripture is the interpretation of the word translated as "pierced." The most ancient translations of the Hebrew texts are the Greek Septuagint,[1] the Aramaic Targums[2] and Latin vulgate versions. These versions of the Bible were translated using very ancient Hebrew manuscripts that were extant in the period 400 B.C.E.-300 C.E. At that time the Hebrew language was diminishing in use, however it was still well understood by the ancient rabbis who translated the Tanakh. The seventy scholars that were chosen to translate the Hebrew manuscripts into Greek were certainly chosen because of their expertise in languages and understanding of scripture.[3]

When we examine these ancient translations of the Tanakh we find that in each case the word in question is translated from Hebrew into the Greek, Syriac or Latin word equivalent to "pierced." The ancient rabbis commissioned to translate the Tanakh into the Septuagint and the ancient Targums were apparently convinced that the word in question was indeed "pierced." The fact that Christian translators (who translated the Hebrew Tanakh

---

[1] The Septuagint; seventy Hebrew and Greek scholars translated the Hebrew Tanakh into Greek beginning in 285 B.C.

[2] Targums: Translated in ~200 B.C.

[3] Some Jewish legends say seventy-two scholars , six from each tribe of Israel, translated it in 285 B.C. The exact amount of time it took to translate the Tanakh (Genesis-Malachi) is not known. Some scholars feel that the Septuagint is flawed in some of its translations. However, it was accepted during the first century C.E.. as a bonafide translation and was used extensively in synagogues and by the common man.

into the Latin Vulgate) translated the same word as pierced, was not an issue at the time. They were simply following what the rabbis had done hundreds of years previously. However, since the "piercing" of Jesus of Nazareth, the translation of this word has become a major point of controversy.

Not only do most contemporary rabbis deny the Messianic application of this verse, some have even stated that Christians fabricated the translation themselves! According to Samuel Levine:[1]

> "That verse of 'they pierced my hands and feet,' which seems to point to Jesus, **is a mistranslation, according to all of the classical Jewish scholars,** who knew Hebrew perfectly. In fact, the Christians have invented a new word in the process, which is still not in the Hebrew dictionary"

Mr. Levine is correct about one thing here. The ancient rabbis knew Hebrew perfectly well. But there is no doubt that the word translated as "pierced" was in their dictionaries because they rendered it that way in the Septuagint and the Targums. Both of these documents were translated some two hundred years before the birth of Jesus.

The Hebrew word which translates as "pierced" is the word "karv", כארו, and was certainly the word those ancient scholars translated. Modern Jewish Bibles translate the word in question as "like a lion." Obviously these are two very different meanings for what should be the same word in the biblical text. So where does this radical difference in rendering come from?

---

[1] *You Take Jesus, I'll Take God*, Samuel Levine, pg. 34, Hamoroh Press, 1980.

The Jewish Publication Society relies on the Massoretic Hebrew text for the translation of their version of the Bible.[1] However, this text is dated to approximately 800-1000 C.E. The writers of the Septuagint, the Targums and the early Christian Bibles relied on much more ancient texts.

The Massoretic text has a completely different word, "kari" כָּאֲרִי, (like a lion), instead of the word "karv" כָּאֲרֿשׁ (pierced) most likely found in the much more ancient texts.

Obviously when you look at the two Hebrew words, כָּאֲרִי and כָּאֲרֿשׁ, we see that they are structurally very similar. The Hebrew letter vav (שׁ) found in "karv" (pierced) is very similar to the letter yod (ֿ) found in the word "kari" (like a lion). Clearly a mistake in copying was possible, but was this change from the ancient text a simple copyist error or the deliberate changing of the text of the book of Psalms?

Was the rejection of Jesus' Messianic claims by the first century rabbis the motive behind the changing of the text as well as its interpretation? We may never know.

Even without this dilemma we find that the ancient rabbinical interpretation of the word in question varies dramatically from modern rabbinical sources. The rabbis who wrote the Talmud and the Midrash interpreted this entire Psalm as Messianic.

In the Yakult Shimoni (#687), a commentary on Psalm 22 we read:

---

[1] This is one of the major publishers of Bibles for the Conservative and Orthodox Jews.

" 'Many dogs have surrounded me', this refers to Haman's sons. 'The assembly of the wicked have enclosed me. They pierced כָּארוּ (karv) my hands and feet.' Rabbi Nehemiah says; **'They pierced my hands and feet in the presence of Ahasuerus.' "**

This commentary shows that the reading "pierced" was accepted by rabbis of that time.

Psalm 22 is also applied to the Messiah in the Midrash Pesikta Rabbat (Piska chapter 36:1-2) as we saw in our discussion of Isaiah 52 and 53.

They Will Look Upon Me Whom They Have Pierced

In the book of Zechariah we find a fascinating prophecy regarding the response of the nation of Israel when they are returned to their land and finally see and recognize their Messiah. God, speaking through Zechariah, stated:

"And I will pour on the house of David and on the inhabitants of Jerusalem the Spirit of grace and supplication; **then they will look on Me whom they have pierced**; they will mourn for him as one mourns for his only son, and grieve for him as one grieves for a firstborn." (Zechariah 12:10-12)

Modern rabbis claim that the person spoken of here *is not* the Messiah, rather a king or priest of either the past or future. However, this very passage is applied to the suffering servant, Messiah Ben Joseph in the Babylonian Talmud, Sukkah 52a. The rabbi asks:

"What is the cause of the mourning [of Zech. 12:10]. **It is well according to him who explains that the cause is the slaying of Messiah, the son of Joseph,**

since that well agrees with the Scriptural verse, 'And
they shall look upon me because they have thrust
him through, and they shall mourn for him as one
mourneth for his only son.'"

In this amazing quote we see that the ancient rabbis
believed that the Messiah would not only be "pierced" or
"thrust through," but that he would also suffer martrydom
("the slaying of Messiah the son of Joseph").

Again we see how the interpretation of prophecy has
changed over the last 1600 years. Was the piercing of the
hands and feet of Jesus of Nazareth, and the thrusting
through of his side by the Roman Guard, the reason for the
change of interpretation of these prophecies? If we are to
argue that the ancient rabbis had a more thorough
understanding of the ancient Hebrew language, we must
accept the ancient views as closest to the true prophetic
meaning.

The Messiah Will Suffer and
Die for the People

The evidence speaks for itself. Throughout most of the
history of Jewish scholarship many of the highly respected
writers of the Talmud and the Midrash (most of whom
were leaders of rabbinical academies) shared a common
belief. The Messiah would be despised, rejected, suffer by
being pierced and ultimately die for the sins of the people.

Consequently, if the twentieth century rabbi or Bible
scholar chooses to cling to the belief that the Messiah will
simply be a man who will not be despised, rejected or
pierced, he will do so in stark contrast to ancient rabbinical
thought and in the face of overwhelming and mounting
evidence to the contrary.

CHAPTER 3

BIRTH, LINEAGE AND
MISSION OF MESSIAH

"For unto us a Child is born, unto us a Son is given;
and the government will be upon his shoulder. And his
name will be called Wonderful, Counselor, Mighty
God, Everlasting Father, Prince of Peace. Of the
increase of his government and peace there will be no
end, upon the throne of David and over his kingdom,
to order it and establish it with judgment and justice
from that time forward, even forever. The zeal of the
LORD of hosts will perform this." (Isaiah 9:6-7)

Woven throughout the Hebrew scriptures we find the
birth, lineage and mission of the Messiah. For nearly 2,000
years the rabbis commented extensively on these scriptures.
As we examine these rabbinical references, as well as new
evidence from the Dead Sea Scrolls, we will get a feel for the
"big picture" regarding the origin and mission of the
Messiah. We will discover that the ancient rabbinical beliefs
are in stark contrast to the contemporary beliefs of most
rabbis and Jewish scholars.

The Preexistence of the Messiah

Before we look at the birth of the Messiah we will look
at the question of his preexistence. As we have seen,
modern rabbis believe that the Messiah is only a man. They
deny the supernatural origin of the Messiah and claim that
he is simply a man of great character, a very charismatic
leader and learned in the Torah, but nothing more than a

human being. However, this has not always been the position of the rabbis. There is abundant evidence in Jewish scholarship that the Messiah would, in fact, be an eternally existent supernatural being, with a supernatural birth, mission and destiny.

Alfred Edersheim, in his book, *The Life and Times of Jesus the Messiah*, Book II, page 175, points out that at one time, most rabbis agreed with this proposition.

"Even in strictly Rabbinic documents, the premundane if not the **eternal existence** of the Messiah, appears as a matter of common belief. Such is the view expressed in the Targum on Isaiah 9:6 and in that on Micah 5:2. But, the Midrash on Proverbs 8:9, expressly mention the Messiah among the seven things created before the world...The name of the Messiah is said to have been created before the world."

In the Septuagint we see other hints as to the eternal existence of the Messiah. In the Septuagint version of Psalm 72, a Messianic Psalm, we find an interesting rendering of verse 5 and 7:

"And he shall continue **as long as the sun**, and before the moon **forever**...In his days shall righteousness spring up; and abundance of peace till the moon be removed."

To ascribe this passage to the life of a mere mortal man is incredible. According to the translators of the Septuagint, the duration of the Messiah's existence is apparently "forever," which implies, by default, that he existed before the creation of the universe.[1]

In the Septuagint rendering of Psalms 110:1-3 we read:

---

[1]Genesis 1:1.

"The Lord said to my Lord, sit thou on my right hand, until I make thine enemies thy footstool. The Lord shall send out a rod of power for thee out of Zion: rule thou in the midst of thine enemies. With thee is dominion in the day of thy power, in the splendours of thy saints: **I have begotten thee from the womb before the morning**" (Before the creation of the Universe).

Finally, in the Septuagint rendering of Micah 5:2 we read of the eternal existence of the Messiah.

" And thou, Bethlehem, house of Ephrathah, art few in number to be reckoned among the thousands of Judah; yet out of thee shall one come forth to me, to be a ruler of Israel; **and his goings forth were from the beginning, even from eternity.**"

It is also notable that in the Babylonian Talmud in Sotah 9b, the Messiah is referred to as:

"being greater than the Patriarchs, higher than Moses, and even loftier than the ministering angels."

The eternal existence of the Messiah, although not universally held by the ancient rabbis, was clearly believed by the ancient Septuagint translators. Furthermore, they, along with some writers of the Talmud, believed the Messiah is a supernatural being whose "goings forth were from the beginning, even from eternity," one who was "loftier than the ministering angels," one who was begotten "from the womb before the morning," one who would "continue as long as the sun, and before the moon forever." To propose and to argue that these prophecies could be fulfilled in the life, ministry and destiny of a mere mortal man is to abandon logic and common sense.

The Birth of the Messiah

"And thou, Bethlehem, house of Ephrathah, art few in
number to be reckoned among the thousands of Judah;
yet out of thee shall one come forth to me, to be a
ruler of Israel; and his goings forth were from the
beginning, even from eternity." (Micah 5:2,
Septuagint)

The city of Bethlehem is perhaps the most famous
village in the world. Among its notable residents were King
David and Jesus of Nazareth. The belief that the Messiah
would come from Bethlehem has its origin in the above
passage. The identity of the "ruler in Israel" born in
Bethlehem can be easily determined by an examination of
the ancient rabbinical sources.

This passage is Messianically applied in the
Targumim,[1] in Pirqe' de Rabbi Eliezer chapter 3, and by
later rabbis.[2]

In the Targum of Jonathan (Targum of the Prophets) we
find this fascinating quote regarding the birth of the
Messiah:

"And you, O Bethlehem Ephrathah, you who were too
small to be numbered among the thousands of the
house of Judah, **from you shall come forth before
Me the Messiah**, to exercise dominion over Israel,
he whose name was mentioned before, from the days
of creation."[3]

---

[1] The Targumim, plural for the Targums, are ancient Aramaic translation
with commentaries interwoven in the text; second century B.C.E.
[2] *The Life and Times of Jesus the Messiah*, Edersheim, Appendix IX.
[3] *The Messiah: An Aramaic Interpretation; The Messianic Exegesis of the
Targum*, Samson H. Levy (Cincinnati: Hebrew Union College Jewish
Institute of Religion, 1974), pg. 92.

Here we see that the Messiah would not only be born in Bethlehem but that his name would exist before the creation of the world.

Born of a Virgin?

"Therefore the Lord himself will give you a sign: Behold, a virgin shall conceive in the womb and shall bring forth a Son, and thou shalt call his name Emmanuel." (Isaiah 7:14, Septuagint version)

The identity of the person in this passage has been a controversy for centuries. The one born of a virgin and named in this passage (Emmanuel, meaning with us is God) is, according to Christian scholars, the Messiah. However, as we saw in chapter one, modern Jewish scholars deny the virgin birth of the Messiah and the Messianic application of this verse. Rabbinical references applying this verse to the Messiah are rare. However, the controversy regarding the identity of the person called, "God with us," begs the question, "If this is not the Messiah, then whom else?" To ascribe such a supernatural birth and title to a mere mortal is ridiculous. Since angels aren't conceived in the womb, they can't qualify. Therefore, the only logical candidate is the Messiah.

There is also a controversy as to the correct translation of the word "Almah," translated "virgin" by the translators of the Septuagint. When confronted with the word "Almah," they translated it into the Greek word "parthenos" meaning an unmarried virgin. This word is derived from the words "parthenia," meaning virginity and the word "agamos," meaning unmarried.

After the advent of Christianity and the claim that Jesus of Nazareth was born of a virgin, the rabbis eventually began to interpret the word "Almah," found in Isaiah 7:14, as a "young woman."

Secondly, the passage says that "The Lord himself will give you *a sign.*" Usually a sign from God is an impressive disruption in the natural flow of things, a supernatural event. Fire from heaven, resurrection from the dead, parting the Red Sea, miraculous healings are typical signs from God. But a "young woman" conceiving and bearing a son?

Although the production of a child from a fertilized egg the size of the head of a pin is impressive, perhaps even a miracle in its own right, such an event could hardly be described as a sign. This same event occurs millions of times every year. Clearly, the event spoken of here is a supernatural conception, a miraculous sign, and an unprecedented event in human history–"Behold, a virgin shall conceive!"

The name Emmanuel[1] means "God with us." Even the 20th century Jewish Publication Society Bible admits that Emmanuel means "with us is God." Was this the Messiah?

Messiah Will Reign
from David's Throne

"For unto us a child is born, unto us a Son is given; And the government will be upon his shoulder; And his name will be called Wonderful, Counselor, Mighty God, Everlasting Father, Prince of Peace." (Isaiah 9:6, NKJ)

"For unto us a child is born, a son is given unto us; And the government is upon his shoulder; And his

---

[1]Also rendered as Immanuel by many scholars.

name is called Pele-joez-El gibbor-abi-ad-sar-shalom.[1] His government shall be great, and of his peace there is no end: it shall be upon the throne of David, and upon his kingdom, to establish it, and to support it with judgment and with righteousness from henceforth and forever. The zeal of the Lord of hosts shall perform this." (Isaiah 9:5-7, JPS, 1917)

In this incredibly beautiful passage we see more revealed about the origin, mission and identity of the Messiah than perhaps any other passage in the Bible.

The Messiah would be born as a child and rule on David's throne, yet he also would be called Wonderful, Counselor, Mighty God, Everlasting Father, Prince of Peace. In many of the writings of the ancient rabbis this passage is specifically applied to the Messiah.[2]

Most modern rabbis reject the Messianic application of this prophecy. In fact, the modern group Jews for Judaism applies this prophecy to Hezekiah, the king of Judah, in the eighth century B.C.E. As we shall see, this opinion has not always been held by the rabbis.

In a book of eighteen beautiful Psalms, called the Psalter of Solomon, written by an unknown Jewish source in 50 B.C.E., Isaiah 9:6-7 is referred to when the writer states of the Messiah:

"He is the king who reigns in the house of David.[3]...He is the son of David, who comes at the

---

[1]This is translated in the footnotes of the Jewish Publication Society Bible as, "Wonderful in counsel is God the Mighty, the Everlasting Father, the ruler of Peace." However, this translation is not a correct one. The text has been manipulated to come up with this translation.

[2]Isaiah 9:6 is applied to the Messiah in the Targum of Isaiah, in the Midrash, Bemidbar Rabbah 11, the Midrash commentary on numbers and in the Babylonian Talmud Siphre', paragraph 42.

[3]Psalter of Solomon, chapter 17:5

time known to God only, to reign over Israel,[1]...**He is Christ the Lord** [2]...He is pure from sin.[3]..He will bring his people the blessings of restoration...and judge the nations, who will be subject to his rule, and behold and own his glory."[4]

The word "Christ" is from the Greek "Christos" which is the translation for the Hebrew word "Mashiyach"– Anointed one–The Messiah!

In this beautiful psalm we see again a supernatural Messianic figure who rules on David's throne, who (in the first century B.C.E.) is called Christ the Lord–an idiom for the Messiah.

Twentieth century Jewish scholar S.A. Horodetsky, writing in "MOZNAIM," a Hebrew periodical, ties the identity of the person who is called Immanuel in Isaiah 7:14 to the individuals spoken of in Isaiah 9:6 and Isaiah 11:1.[5,6]

"Behold the almah shall conceive, and bear a son, and shall call his name Immanuel" (reference to Isaiah 7:14).

Horodetsky continues:

"For unto us a Child is born, unto us a Son is given; and the government rests on his shoulders: And his name will be called Wonderful, Counselor, Mighty God, Eternal Father, Prince of Peace." (reference to Isaiah 9:6.)

[1]ibid chapter 5:3
[2]ibid chapter 5:36
[3]ibid chapter 5:41
[4]ibid chapter 5:25-35
[5]S.A. Horodetsky, in MOZNAIM ("Balances" or "Scales") V01 1, No.10; Nov-Dec., 1929.
[6]This discussion is adapted from *The Messianic Hope*, Arthur Kac, Baker Books, pg. 40-41.

"There shall come forth a Rod from the stem of Jesse, and a Branch shall grow out of his roots" (Isaiah 11:1).[1]

Speaking of the individual identified in these three prophecies, Horodetsky states:

"He is singled out and more marvelous than any of the holy children in the Bible. When the Judean kingdom was in danger of being destroyed Isaiah prophesied in God's name, saying: '**Behold, the almah conceives and gives birth to a son and calls his name Immanuel.**' About the quality and character of this child the prophet says laconically: 'Butter and honey shall he eat, despising the evil and choosing the good.' Isaiah prophesies again about **the same child, but calls him by a different name, namely, 'A child is born unto us, a son is given unto us; and the government rests upon his shoulders: and his name shall be called, Wonderful, Counselor, Mighty God, Eternal Father, Prince of Peace,'** etc., etc. In another place, the prophet relates in more clear and more detailed words the descent, character and mission of this child (Isaiah 11). **All these descriptions, namely, Immanuel, Wonderful, Counselor, Root of Jesse's stock, are linked together by one, namely, Immanuel.** This last name is the principal name of the child, so much so that in Isaiah 8:8 the whole land of Judah is called the land of Immanuel."

It is startling to see a Hebrew periodical admit that the figure spoken of in these three are indeed the same person. The fact that these three passages were believed to be Messianic by the ancient rabbis in the Psalter of Solomon

---

[1] The translation of these three passages is taken from Ninteenth century German Semitic scholar, Dr. Franz Delitzsch, in his work entitled *The Prophecies Of Isaiah* and referenced by Horodetsky.

and other writings is conclusive.[1] The Messiah, the one
whose name is "God with us," "Wonderful," "Counselor,"
"Mighty God," "Prince of Peace," and "Christ the Lord"
will be born of a virgin, carry the government upon his
shoulders and rule upon the throne of David forever.

He Would Be a King

"Behold, the days are coming," says the LORD, "That
I will raise to David a Branch of righteousness; a King
shall reign and prosper, and execute judgment and
righteousness in the earth. In his days Judah will be
saved, and Israel will dwell safely; now this is his name
by which he will be called: THE LORD OUR
RIGHTEOUSNESS." (Jeremiah 23:5-6)

This beautiful promise of the coming redemption of
Judah was clearly believed to be Messianic by the ancient
rabbis. This passage presents one of the highest views of
the Messiah in the entire Hebrew Bible. Not only would he
be a king from the lineage of David, he would also be a
savior and his name would be "The LORD our
Righteousness"! This passage is Messianically applied in
the Targum, Talmud and Midrash.

The Targum of Jeremiah has an interpretation:

"I will raise up for David the Messiah the just."

This is one of the passages from which, according to the
ancient rabbis, one of the names of Messiah is derived,
"Jehovah our Righteousness."[2] That is, they believed that

---

[1]Isaiah 11:1 is applied to the Messiah in the Targum of Isaiah, and in the
Babylonian Talmud, Sanhedrin 93b and in the Yakult (vol.1, pg. 24).
[2] Talmud Babha Bathra 75b, Midrash on Psalm 21:1, Proverbs 19:21,
Lamentations 1:16. All of these sources refer to Messiah being called
"Jehovah our Righteousness."

the Messiah was in some way a literal manifestation of Jehovah himself!

A King on a donkey:

> "Rejoice greatly, O daughter of Zion; proclaim it aloud, O daughter of Jerusalem; behold, the King is coming to thee, just, and a Savior; he is meek and riding on an ass, and a young foal." (Zechariah 9:9, Septuagint version)

Since the day Jesus of Nazareth rode into the east gate of Jerusalem on a donkey, Christians have pointed to this prophecy as Messianic and being fulfilled in Jesus. However, modern rabbis deny that the Messiah will be lowly and come to Israel on a donkey. Yet, Zechariah the prophet, prophesying in the days of the Second Temple, declared that a savior would come into the city of Jerusalem in just this way. When we examine the writings of the ancient rabbis, we find they believed it to be a prophecy regarding the Messiah.

In the Babylonian Talmud Sanhedrin 99a we read:

> "Rabbi Hillel said: there shall be no Messiah for Israel, because they have already enjoyed him in the days of Hezekiah. Rabbi Joseph said: 'may God forgive him for saying so. Now, when did Hezekiah flourish? During the First Temple. Yet Zechariah, prophesying in the days of the second, proclaimed, 'rejoice greatly O daughter of Zion; shout, O daughter of Jerusalem; behold, thy King cometh unto thee! He is just, and having salvation; lowly, and riding upon an ass, and upon a colt the foal of an ass.' "

In this incredible quote from the Babylonian Talmud, we see Rabbi Joseph proclaiming that the Messiah could not have come during the days of Hezekiah, because

Hezekiah lived during the days of the First Temple. He goes on to validate the Messianic application of this prophecy in declaring that the Messiah would be lowly and come to Jerusalem riding on a donkey.

In the Babylonian Talmud, there is a fascinating commentary on the "Son of Man" spoken of in Daniel 7:13.

"I was watching in the night visions, and behold, One like the Son of Man, coming with the clouds of heaven! He came to the Ancient of Days, and they brought him near before him." (Daniel 7:13)

This passage is curiously explained in the Talmud, Sanhedrin 98a:

"If Israel behaved worthily, the Messiah would come in the clouds of heaven, if otherwise, humble riding on a donkey."

The Talmud writer clearly ties the "Son of Man" in Daniel with the lowly King in Zechariah 9:9.

In another Talmudic passage, during a discourse about the Messiah's redemption the Talmud writer states:

"If one sees an ass in a dream, he may hope for salvation, as it says, 'Behold thy King cometh unto thee; he is triumphant and victorious, lowly and riding upon an ass.' "[1]

The Mission of the Messiah

Woven among the passages we have just examined we find a number of facets of the mission of the Messiah.

---

[1]Babylonian Talmud, Bereshith 56b.

According to these passages, Messiah would be a savior who would execute judgment and righteousness in the earth while reigning upon the throne of David. A close examination of the Hebrew scriptures reveals that this only scratches the surface of the mission of the Messiah.

In the book of Isaiah we find that the Messiah is prophesied to have a tremendous ministry of spiritual and physical healing.

"The Spirit of the Lord GOD is upon Me, because the LORD has anointed Me to preach good tidings to the poor; he has sent Me to heal the brokenhearted, to proclaim liberty to the captives, and the opening of the prison to those who are bound; to proclaim the acceptable year of the LORD, and the day of vengeance of our God; to comfort all who mourn, to console those who mourn in Zion, to give them beauty for ashes, the oil of joy for mourning, the garment of praise for the spirit of heaviness; that they may be called trees of righteousness, the planting of the LORD, that he may be glorified." (Isaiah 61:1-3)

"In that day the deaf shall hear the words of the book, and the eyes of the blind shall see out of obscurity and out of darkness. The humble also shall increase their joy in the LORD, and the poor among men shall rejoice in the Holy One of Israel." (Isaiah 29:18-19)

"Then the eyes of the blind shall be opened, and the ears of the deaf shall be unstopped. Then the lame shall leap like a deer, and the tongue of the dumb sing. For waters shall burst forth in the wilderness, and streams in the desert." (Isaiah 35:5-6)

These verses represent some of the most beautiful verses regarding the mission of the Messiah in the entire Bible. Clearly, in the healing of the deaf, blind and the lame, these prophecies speak of a mission which is supernatural, a ministry which could hardly be accomplished through an ordinary man. Many ancient rabbinical sources indicate the belief that the performance of these miraculous signs is accomplished by none other than the Messiah.[1]

Jeremiah the prophet was a witness to the destruction of Israel in the seventh century B.C. Prophet after prophet was sent to the nation to warn them of the coming catastrophe, which was sanctioned by God because the people had broken the covenant with him. Many of the people, including their leaders, had fallen into idol worship, sexual immorality, and they had failed to rest the land as required in the law of Moses. Consequently, the nation of Israel was destroyed and the people taken captive for seventy years, exactly the number of years they owed God in the resting of the land. In the midst of this disaster, God speaks through Jeremiah and promises a new covenant to the nation of Israel, a covenant that the ancient rabbis believed would be brought by the Messiah.

"Behold, the days are coming," says the LORD, "when **I will make a new covenant with the house of Israel and with the house of Judah**; not according to the covenant that I made with their fathers in the day that I took them by the hand to bring them out of the land of Egypt, My covenant which they broke, though I was a husband to them," says the LORD. "But this is the covenant that I will make with the house of Israel: After those days, says the LORD, **I will put My law in their minds, and write it on their hearts; and I will be their God, and they shall be My people.** No more shall every man teach his neighbor, and every man his brother, saying, 'Know the LORD,' for they all shall know Me, from the least of them to the greatest of them," says the LORD.

---

[1] See Midrash on Lamentations, chapter 3:49, Yakult i.78 and 178a, Midrash on Genesis chapter 95 and Midrash on Psalms 146:8. These verses are specifically applied to the Messiah in these documents

"For I will forgive their iniquity, and their sin I will remember no more."[1] (Jeremiah 31:31-34)

In this heart-warming passage we see a vivid picture of a loving father bending in reconciliation to his disobedient children. Here Jeremiah proclaims a message of hope and restoration during the Messianic Kingdom. This new covenant was to be a covenant of the heart, as opposed to one on stone tablets. This new covenant was to be a covenant whereby man would relate to God in faith and not with the works of the law.

This verse was applied to the Messiah by ancient rabbis in many places.[2] This new covenant relationship was to be a major accomplishment of the Messiah.

Finally, the Bible speaks of a Messianic mission to the gentiles:

"And in that day there shall be a **Root of Jesse**, who shall stand as a banner to the people; for the gentiles shall seek him, and his resting place shall be glorious." (Isaiah 11:10)

To the ancient Jewish mind the gentiles were viewed as filthy dogs, sub-human, unclean, made by God only to provide fuel for hell! So when Isaiah penned this prophecy, many must have thought he had lost his mind. However, as time progressed, the rabbis eventually viewed the conversion of the gentiles (called proselytes) as a rabbinical and Messianic mission. The root of Jesse is recognized even today as an idiom for the Messiah.[3]

---

[1]These verses are all applied to the Messiah in Yakult vol. 1 pg. 76 and vol. 2 pg. 54b and 66d.
[2]See Yakult vol. 1, pg. 196c; 78c; vol. 2. pg. 54b and 66d.
[3]Messianically applied in the Targum. The Midrash on Psalm 21:1 declares the person referred to in Isaiah 11:10 is the Messiah.

In our brief examination of the Hebrew scriptures and their ancient rabbinical interpretations, we have found many specific indicators and requirements that the rabbis were expecting to find fulfilled in the resumé of any man that might claim the title of Messiah. Yet, this is only a partial list of the hundreds of passages recognized as Messianic by the ancient rabbis.[1]

As we progress through this book we will see many more of these hallmarks of the Messianic resumé. However, even with the prophecies we have examined so far we are in a position to ask whether Jesus of Nazareth (or anyone else for that matter) has fulfilled the biblical Messianic composite that the ancient rabbis were expecting.

---

[1] For a complete list see *The Life and Times of Jesus the Messiah*, Edersheim, Alfred, Appendix IX.

CHAPTER 4

THE LOWLY CARPENTER

The Resumé of the Messiah

Up to this point we have been able to gather a fairly clear composite picture of the ancient expectations regarding the birth, lineage, mission, character and destiny of the Messiah. Any individual that would claim to be the Messiah must fulfill each and every one of these prophecies in order to merit any serious consideration.

Among the many hundreds of Messianic prophecies in the Tanakh, we have found that early scholars believed the Messiah would be a supernatural being, one **"whose goings forth were from the beginning, even from eternity."** He would leave the timeless realm of eternity to be **"born of a virgin"** among **"the line of David"** in the city of Bethlehem. We have seen that **"His name will be called Wonderful, Counselor, Mighty God, Everlasting Father, Prince of Peace."** He would be a **"light to the gentiles."** He would **"bring a new covenant to the Jews...heal the sick...** **"proclaim liberty to the captives"**...Yet, **"He is just, and having salvation; lowly, and riding upon an ass."** Finally, he would reign **"upon the throne of David"** and...**"the government will be upon his shoulder."** Regarding the duration of his kingdom we read that... **"Of the increase of his government and peace there will be no end...to support it with judgment and with righteousness from henceforth and forever."**

51

Finally, we established that despite these accomplishments he would be despised, rejected and die for the sins of the people.

How can such a set of paradoxical destinies be accomplished in the life of a single individual? How could the Messiah be despised and rejected and yet rule on the throne of David in power and righteousness forever and ever? These questions surely troubled the ancient writers of the Midrashim as they troubled me. The solution, as we will see, is a startling plan of God foreordained before the foundations of the earth.

The Candidates

In the last 3500 years there have been a number of men who have claimed to be the Messiah. To this very day, on television talk shows, in books, magazines and even churches, people continue to make this claim. Yet, there is only one candidate whose impact has spanned the reaches of the globe, the test of time and can claim billions of followers. That is, of course, the Messianic claim of Jesus of Nazareth.

Of course, modern rabbis, with their radically different view of Messianic prophecy, deny that anyone in history has come forward who fits the required composite picture of the Messiah. However, our purpose so far has been to evaluate biblical prophecy and the views of the ancient rabbis (who clearly had a better understanding of the ancient Hebrew language) in order to get a composite picture of the Messiah and determine whether anyone in history has come forward with a claim that fulfilled the criteria *they* set forth.

When we look through history we find no shortage of men who desired to claim the title of Messiah.

During the procuratorship of Cuspium Fadus (44 C.E.), there was a man by the name of Thadeus who declared he was the Messiah, and according to Josephus:

> "...many were deluded by his words. However, Fadus did not permit them to make any advantage of his wild attempt, but sent a troop of horsemen out against them who, falling upon them unexpectedly, slew many of them and took many of them alive. They also took Thadeus alive and cut off his head and carried it to Jerusalem." [1]

According to twentieth century Rabbi Abba Hillel Silver,[2] the Romans were extremely severe on Thadeus, because he:

> "...entertained Messianic notions of himself or announced himself as the Messiah. The Messianic hope, of course, always implied the overthrow of the Roman power in Palestine."

Rabbi Silver goes on to describe the first century as one of numerous outbreaks of Messianic movements. However, virtually all of the first century Messianic movements ended in disaster. According to Josephus, during the first half of the first century:

> "...there were such men as deceived and deluded the people under the pretense of divine inspiration, but were for procuring innovations and changes of the government; and these prevailed with the multitude to act like mad men, and went before them into the

---

[1] *Antiquities of the Jews*, Book 20:5:1.
[2] *A History of Messianic Speculation in Israel*, Rabbi Abba Hillel Silver, Page 5.

wilderness, as pretending that God would there show them the signals of liberty; but Felix [the Roman Procurator] thought the procedure was to be the beginnings of a revolt; so he sent some horsemen and footmen, both armed, who destroyed a great number of them."

In the second century C.E., there was the Jewish revolt against the Roman government, commonly called, the Bar Kochba revolt, led by Simeon Bar Kosba, but popularly called Bar Kochba.

This revolt flared up in 132-135 C.E. because the Roman emperor, Hadrian, decided to integrate the Jews into the empire and build a temple to Jupiter Capitolinus over the ruins of the previously destroyed Jewish temple. According to historic evidence, Simeon Bar Kosba led the revolution and was reputedly hailed as the Messiah and the greatest rabbi of all time by rabbi Akiba. Simeon Bar Kosba was given the name Bar Kochba, which means 'son of the star,' a Messianic allusion, by the Jewish leaders of the day. The revolution ended in defeat and Bar Kochba was eventually killed in 135 C.E. The remaining remnant of the Jewish army was then crushed by men of the Roman tenth legion.

After the Bar Kochba disaster, the rabbis began to speculate that the coming of the Messiah would be far off in the future. Some even declared that he had already come but had been missed. The great rabbi Hillel stated:

"Israel no longer need expect the Messiah, for he was already consumed in the days of Hezekiah."[1]

Rabbi Silver states that:

---

[1]Babylonian Talmud, Sanhedrin 99a

"Following the frustration of the Messianic hope in the second century, the next Messianic date seems to have been generally, though not exclusively, placed about four hundred years after the destruction [of the Second Temple], somewhere in the fifth century. The rabbis no longer pointed to a date in the near future, but projected it into a relatively distant future."[1]

Rabbi Silver explains that the Messianic disasters of the first and second centuries C.E. forced the rabbis to push for an end to Messianic date setting and promoting favorite candidates. We will look at ancient rabbinical beliefs on the time of the coming the Messiah in a later chapter.

In modern times, there have been a number of claimants to the Messianic title. The world is all too familiar with the tragic ending of the Branch Davidian cult, lead by self-proclaimed Messiah, David Koresh. His Messianic claim ended in the same way so many other such movements have ended over the centuries. The leader is either killed or arrested and the followers disband.

The Lowly Carpenter

In the entire history of Messianic movements, there is only one man who has made a permanent mark on virtually the entire world with such a claim. His name is Jesus of Nazareth. What was different about the Messianic claims of Jesus of Nazareth? Why did his Messianic following continue to grow and expand in the face of tremendous persecution throughout the world? Did he fulfill the biblical expectations of the first century Jews and therefore deserve the title "Messiah," or was he a deceiver, charlatan or a lunatic? Worse yet, is the story of Jesus of Nazareth

---

[1]*A History of Messianic Speculation in Israel*, Rabbi Abba Hillel Silver, Pg.25.

simply a well-crafted hoax, designed by men with political and financial gain in mind? What are the reasons for this lasting effect on world history and the lives of billions of people? Why was he accepted as the Messiah by thousands of Jews within just a few weeks of his death? What set him apart?

In the next several chapters we will attempt to answer these questions by holding up the biblical and early rabbinical expectations for the Messiah and compare them with the birth, life, ministry and destiny of Jesus of Nazareth.

The Paradox

The impact that this one man has had on the world is unparalleled and unprecedented in history. How can we explain the tremendously divisive reaction that the world has had to this man Jesus?

On the one hand, Jesus has been worshipped by billions as God in human flesh, yet, on the other hand, despised and rejected by billions, including the majority of the Jewish leadership of the last 2,000 years.

To gain clarity on this issue we need to look at the development of the Messianic expectations that the common man and the Jewish leadership had during the time of Jesus of Nazareth. So far, we have examined selected prophecies from the Hebrew Scriptures, as well as their ancient interpretations, to get the composite Messianic picture that the rabbis held to during the time of Jesus. This view, which we could call the "biblical view," was not necessarily the "popular view" held by the people during that time period.

The Mood of First Century Israel

The nation of Israel, like no other nation in history, has suffered tremendous persecution and dislocation from their land numerous times during the past 3,500 years. When Jesus of Nazareth entered the world scene the Jews had been back into the land for over 500 years. Yet, they still remained under the dominant hand of a foreign power.

The Jewish people had been taken captive in 606 B.C.E. by the Babylonians, under King Nebuchadnezzar, and were allowed to return to the land seventy years later in 537 B.C.E.[1] When they returned to Israel, they rebuilt the city of Jerusalem and the Temple.

The next 500 years were tumultuous times for the Jews. They suffered under the Medo-Persian, Greek and finally the Roman empires. In 165 B.C.E., Antiochus Epiphanes slaughtered a pig in the "Holy of Holies" of the Second Temple and incited the tremendous Macabean revolt of that time.

From that time forward, Jewish zealots strengthened their resolve to end foreign domination. A growing movement developed to free Israel from the grips of the Romans, and in concert with this, an expectation arose that the Messiah would come and defeat the Romans militarily and return Israel to the glory it saw under the reign of King David. Their desire to be freed from the Roman yoke caused them to look for a leader who would fulfill the Davidic ruling and reigning Messianic prophecies. The other biblical view of a humble, suffering servant Messiah, riding into Jerusalem on a donkey, was put on the back burner in

---

[1] See *The Babylon Report* by Chuck Missler and Hal Lindsey for a detailed discussion of the chronology of this period. Koinonia House, PO Box D, CDA, Idaho, 83816-0317

the minds of the first century Jews. Because of their suffering, and despite the abundant Messianic clues in the scriptures, the majority of the people, including the leadership of the Jews, developed a non-biblical view of the Messiah, that is, a one-sided ruling and reigning Messiah.

The frustration of the Jewish nation reached its peak with the removal of the Jewish right to impose capital punishment in the year 6-7 C.E.

At that time, Herod Archelaus, the son of Herod the Great, was banished by the Roman government. In his place was appointed the first Roman Procurator, Caponius, who was given authority over the nation of Israel.

The authority of the Sanhedrin was abruptly and severely restricted, including their right to adjudicate and carry out capital cases. Their national identity and last remaining remnant of sovereignty was crushed. The Sanhedrin, the ruling body in the early first century, was now largely ceremonial and was subject to the whims of the Roman empire.

It was with this backdrop of nationalism and despair that Jesus of Nazareth sprung onto the scene. As we shall see, Messianic expectations were extremely high during the first half of the first century C.E. However, the people were "set up" to receive a Messiah that was more a product of their popular expectations and hopes rather than the biblical Messiah portrayed by the many prophets who had come before him.

The Two "Veins" of Prophecy

In our examination of the Hebrew scriptures, we saw that there are two "veins" of biblical prophecy that present the mission and destiny of the Messiah.

On the one hand, we saw that the Messiah would be a supernatural being who would rule and reign in Israel upon the throne of David forever and ever. With the government upon his shoulders, he would bring about everlasting righteousness and peace. Yet, on the other hand, we have seen that there is another vein of prophecy that runs throughout the entire Tanakh, one which proclaims that the Messiah would be lowly, even to the point of entering Jerusalem on a donkey, that he would be despised and rejected by men, that he would be pierced or thrust through and that, ultimately, he would "pour out his soul unto death" or be "cut off" for the sins of the people.

According to the ancient rabbis, through Messiah's death, salvation would come to the people and nation of Israel.[1] And, we have seen that this outpouring of God's grace would be extended even to the gentile world.

Jewish scholars of ancient and modern times have had great difficulty in uniting these two "veins" of prophecy in the life of a single individual. Therefore, early in rabbinical Judaism, we saw that the Messiah was split into two distinct personalities: Messiah Ben Joseph, the suffering servant, and Messiah Ben David, the ruling and reigning Messiah.

However, as we will discover, recent manuscript discoveries in the Dead Sea Scrolls reveal that this belief in two Messiahs was not universally accepted in Judaism.

---

[1] See the discussion on Isaiah 53, chapter two.

There is evidence from the Tanakh, the Talmud and the writings of the Qumran community, that there would in fact be only one Messiah!

So, we must ask, does the life, ministry and destiny of the carpenter from Nazareth fulfill the two "veins" of prophecy found in biblical Messianic composite?

The Birth and Lineage of Jesus

"But you, Bethlehem Ephrathah, though you are little among the thousands of Judah, yet out of you shall come forth to me one to be ruler of Israel, whose goings forth have been from old, from everlasting." (Micah 5:2)

"And it came to pass in those days that a decree went out from Caesar Augustus that all the world should be registered. This census first took place while Quirinius was governing Syria. So all went to be registered everyone to his own city. And Joseph also went up from Galilee, out of the city of Nazareth into Judea, to the city of David, which is called Bethlehem, because he was of the house and lineage of David, to be registered with Mary, his betrothed wife, who was with child." (Luke 2:1)

For over 2500 years virtually every rabbi has believed that the Messiah would be born in Bethlehem. In the New Testament we find the story of Joseph and Mary going to the city of Bethlehem to register for taxation.

Mary was due to give birth to Jesus at any time. However, the Messiah needed to be born in the city of David, Bethlehem. Joseph and Mary were living quietly in Nazareth. "How will the Messiah be born in Bethlehem?" they must have thought to themselves. As the time drew near for the baby Jesus to be born, the solution was quite unexpected.

God is able to direct the decisions and the paths of kings and peasants in order to accomplish his will. So, Caesar Augustus made the decree that everyone should be taxed. Since Joseph and Mary were of the line of David, they were required to go to their family's town of origin, Bethlehem of Judea. No doubt Joseph and Mary marveled at the method God used to return them to Bethlehem and thus fulfill the prophecy.

Behold the Virgin!

"Therefore, the Lord himself shall give you a sign; behold, a virgin shall conceive in the womb, and shall bring forth a son, and thou shalt call his name Emmanuel." (Isaiah 7:14, Septuagint Version)

In chapter three we saw evidence that the Messiah, Emmanuel (meaning "with us is God"), was to be born supernaturally of a virgin. The New Testament declares that Jesus of Nazareth was born of a virgin named Mary.

"Now the birth of Jesus Christ was as follows: After his mother Mary was betrothed to Joseph, before they came together, she was found with child of the Holy Spirit." (Matthew 1:18)

Today, modern Jewish scholars deny that the Messiah is to be born of a virgin. They, along with skeptics and atheists, laugh at the idea of someone being virgin born. And yet, according to the Bible, and at least some Jewish scholars, this is how the Messiah would come into the world.

To be fair, believing that the Messiah would be born of a virgin is no less difficult than believing Genesis 1:1:

"In the beginning God created the heavens and the earth."

If you can believe that God made the universe, then a virgin birth is a snap. In fact, it may even be within the reach of modern genetic engineering!

By simply combining the chromosomes found in two human eggs into one, we would have, in theory, the necessary genetic information for a human female! No one, however, has figured out how to "engineer" a male using only a virgin's chromosomes. Clearly, for this, a miracle is required. And that is just what the prophet said would happen, "the Lord himself shall give you "*a sign*," an unprecedented supernatural action.

Line of David

"Behold, the days are coming," says the LORD, "That I will raise to David a Branch of righteousness; a King shall reign and prosper, and execute judgment and righteousness in the earth. In his days Judah will be saved, and Israel will dwell safely; now this is his name by which he will be called: THE LORD OUR RIGHTEOUSNESS." (Jeremiah 23:5-6)

We saw in our study of the lineage of the Messiah that he would come from the "house of David."[1] The New Testament documents record the genealogies for Jesus in the opening chapter of the book of Matthew and in the book of Luke, chapter 3. In both of these genealogies, the writers are extremely careful to demonstrate the Davidic

---

[1]Isaiah 9:6; Isaiah 11:10; Jeremiah 23:5-6.

line of Jesus because they knew that any candidate for the Messiah must be able to demonstrate such a heritage.

Modern rabbis continue to believe that the Messiah will be a son of David, from the tribe of Judah. However, this presents a rather severe difficulty for anyone claiming to be the Messiah. There have been no complete genealogies in existence since the destruction of Jerusalem and the Second Temple in 70 C.E. Prior to that time, almost any Jewish person could confidently trace his genealogy all the way back to Abraham. However, today, no one on earth can prove with certainty that his lineage goes back to David or any of the tribes of Israel. Any Messianic candidate would have an impossible task establishing, with 100 percent certainty, that he is from the lineage required.

Scripture consistently teaches that God leaves nothing to chance. He does not work in approximations or in a haphazard manner. It is, therefore, highly significant that the genealogies were all lost or destroyed at the time of the destruction of the Second Temple.

Is the loss of the genealogies an indicator that the Messiah arrived prior to 70 C.E.? Could it be that the time for the coming of the Messiah has passed? As we shall see, there were ancient rabbis who believed this was so.

The Message and Ministry of Jesus

At about the age of thirty, in the city of Nazareth, Jesus returned to the synagogue he attended as a youth and read this quote from Isaiah.

"The spirit of the Lord God is upon Me, because the Lord has anointed Me to preach good tidings to the poor; he has sent Me to heal the brokenhearted, to proclaim liberty to the captives, and the opening of the prison to those who are bound; to proclaim the acceptable year of the Lord,..." (Isaiah 61:1-2)

Jesus closed the book and gave it back to the attendant. The eyes of all who were in the synagogue were fixed on him. Then Jesus said, "Today this scripture is fulfilled in your hearing."[1]

Jesus was speaking to a crowd that had known him since he was a child in Nazareth. There was no doubt in the minds of the people what Jesus was claiming. It was well known that this was a prophecy of the Messiah, and Jesus was proclaiming that he was the fulfillment of this prophecy!

The people began to ask among themselves, "Is this not Joseph and Mary's son?" Then Jesus said to them, "Assuredly I say to you, no prophet is accepted in his own country." Because of this radical claim, the people of Nazareth became enraged and attempted to kill Jesus.

So began the ministry of Jesus of Nazareth.

The reaction of this crowd was in many ways characteristic of the reaction of crowds today when confronted with the claims of Jesus Christ. From the time he began his ministry, he was the most challenging and controversial figure ever to walk the face of the earth. As we examine the claims of Jesus we will discover why his claims caused great division among the people, as they continue to do, even to the present day.

The message of Jesus was in many ways unexpected and unwanted by the nation of Israel. Their desire for a powerful military leader, one who would lead them out of Roman bondage, superseded the obvious biblical prophecies

---

[1]Luke 4:21.

of a meek and lowly suffering servant Messiah. Therefore, the majority of the Jewish leadership, and the people in general, were caught off guard by the message and ministry of this carpenter from Galilee. And the majority rejected him. However, history tells us that he was also embraced by thousands of Jews of his time.

As we will see, at almost every turn Jesus confounded his disciples and frustrated and offended the Jewish leadership with his conduct or his message.

The Traditions of Men

Throughout the New Testament records we find Jesus orchestrating his actions or message in a way that seemed to test or irritate the Pharisees. This is most evident in his disregard for "the traditions of men." The Pharisees had developed many traditions regarding the "correct" observance of the law given through Moses. The problem was that they often elevated their traditions to the level of the law of God. Many times Jesus pointed out that their traditions were in vain, and not equal in authority to the law of God. In fact, they were often in direct contradiction to the clear teaching of the word of God.

Jesus and the I.R.S.

During the life of Jesus, he was known to eat with sinners and tax collectors.[1] This was pointed out by the Pharisees with righteous indignation.

> "And so it was, as Jesus sat at the table in the house, that behold, many tax collectors and sinners came and sat down with him and his disciples. And when the

---

[1]Luke 5:30.

Pharisees saw it, they said to his disciples, 'Why does
your Teacher eat with tax collectors and sinners?' But
when Jesus heard that, He said to them, 'Those who
are well have no need of a physician, but those who
are sick. But go and learn what this means: 'I desire
mercy and not sacrifice.' For I did not come to call
the righteous, but sinners, to repentance." (Matthew
9:10-13)

Jesus was not interested in pleasing men. He had a
mission. If, in the accomplishment of that mission (bringing
sinners to repentance and salvation), he offended the
leadership, then so be it.

The Pharisees had a belief that eating with the tax
collectors and sinners was an act that would defile one in
the sight of God. However, Jesus points out to the
Pharisees that he came specifically for sinners. He then
quotes Hosea 6:6 which states: "I desire mercy and not
sacrifice." Jesus was pointing out that their traditions,
which usually involved a self righteous display of
deprivation or "good works," were not an acceptable way
to God.

Jesus frequently stated that no one could obtain a
righteous standing before God by following such traditions.
This teaching was a cornerstone to his message and
ministry and laid the foundation for his disciples to
understand the ultimate message of the ministry of Jesus.
Salvation, a right standing with God, could only be obtained
by faith alone, not by even the most sincere practice of
good religious works.

On another day the Pharisees "caught" the disciples of
Jesus breaking one of their traditions and they challenged
him, saying:

" 'Why do Your disciples transgress the tradition of the elders? For they do not wash their hands when they eat bread.' But he [Jesus] answered and said to them, 'Why do you also transgress the commandment of God because of your tradition?'...Hypocrites! Well did Isaiah prophesy about you, saying: 'These people draw near to Me with their mouth, and honor Me with their lips, but their heart is far from Me. And in vain they worship Me, **teaching as doctrines the commandments of men.**' Then he called the multitude and said to them, '**Hear and understand: Not what goes into the mouth defiles a man**; but what comes out of the mouth, this defiles a man.' Then his disciples came and said to him, 'Do You know that the Pharisees were offended when they heard this saying?' " (Matthew 15:2-3, 8-12)

The response of his disciples is hilarious: "Do You know that the Pharisees were offended when they heard this saying?" No kidding. Very perceptive.

Jesus had just pointed out to the Pharisees that their entire system of relating to God, including their entire world view and their system of works, done in an effort to be acceptable in the sight of God, was worthless!

Not only that, he stated that their traditions and system of "good works" had led them far from God and had made them hypocrites!

"Woe to you, Scribes and Pharisees-hypocrites"

Later in the ministry of Jesus, he took direct aim at the duplicity of the scribes and Pharisees. With both barrels loaded, he gave them a tongue lashing that must have spread throughout Jerusalem in no time:

"Then Jesus spoke to the multitudes and to his disciples, saying: 'The scribes and the Pharisees sit in

Moses' seat. Therefore whatever they tell you to observe, that observe and do, but do not do according to their works; for they say, and do not do...But all their works they do to be seen by men. They make their phylacteries broad and enlarge the borders of their garments. They love the best places at feasts, the best seats in the synagogues, ...But woe to you, scribes and Pharisees, hypocrites! For you shut up the kingdom of heaven against men; for you neither go in yourselves, nor do you allow those who are entering to go in...Woe to you, scribes and Pharisees, hypocrites! For you devour widows' houses, and for a pretense make long prayers. Therefore you will receive greater condemnation...Woe to you, scribes and Pharisees, hypocrites! For you cleanse the outside of the cup and dish, but inside they are full of extortion and self-indulgence...Woe to you, scribes and Pharisees, hypocrites! For you are like white washed tombs which indeed appear beautiful outwardly, but inside are full of dead men's bones and all uncleanness." (Matthew 23:1-3, 5-6, 13-14, 25, 27)

"You are of your father the devil, and the desires of your father you want to do. He was a murderer from the beginning, and does not stand in the truth, because there is no truth in him. When he speaks a lie, he speaks from his own resources, for he is a liar and the father of it." (John 8:44)

The words of the Sunday school Jesus, meek and mild with a lamb wrapped around his neck? Hardly!

Jesus struck right to the heart of these men, pointing out their evil motives, and declaring that they were like tombs. The outside was clean, yet, inside they were filthy and evil. No wonder they wanted Jesus dead!

In this discourse Jesus points out to the gathered crowds a number of hypocritical flaws of the Sanhedrin.

Apparently Jesus wanted these impurities to be known by the common man.

Jesus told the people that they should do as their leaders told them, but don't follow their example. He points out that they love the attention and admiration of the people, more than the admiration of God.

However, more harmful than any of these statements was Jesus' claim that the scribes and Pharisees were keeping people from the kingdom of God.

> "But woe to you, scribes and Pharisees, hypocrites! For you shut up the kingdom of heaven against men; for you neither go in yourselves, nor do you allow those who are entering to go in." (Matthew 23:13)

Although there may have been some in the audience who didn't understand this statement, the scribes and Pharisees knew exactly what he was charging.

When the people of Israel would go to the Temple of God to offer an animal sacrifice as an atonement for their sins, they would have to have their animal inspected by a Temple Priest. If even the slightest flaw was found on the animal, they would be directed to purchase one of the "Temple certified" animals that were sold at up to three to four times the normal price. Guess who operated these booths? That's right, the priests under the authority of the Sadducees (a sect of first century Judaism).

When Jesus of Nazareth spoke these words, he was posing a severe threat to their pocket-books, not to mention their standing in the community. As far as the Sadducees were concerned, this kind of discourse was a blatant "in your face" challenge to their authority to govern the people and it hardened their resolve to rid the nation of Jesus of Nazareth.

This guy was radical. He seemed to offend and upset the apple cart at every turn. Could a man of such manner be the Messiah?

Salvation by Faith, Not Works!

Perhaps the central theme of the message of Jesus of Nazareth was that a man's salvation was through his faith in God, and not by his ability to "be good." Jesus declared that a relationship with God must be a right internal response of the heart, not an external obedience to a list of directives. The tradition of strict legalism, manifested in the fanatical adherence to the laws of God as well as the "traditions of men," was insufficient to obtain a righteous standing before God. This teaching of Jesus was so contrary to the prevailing religious mind set that it caught virtually everyone off guard.

Early in the ministry of Jesus he met a Samaritan woman at a well. He proclaimed to her that the kingdom of God was spiritual and that those who worship God must do so in spirit and not by the performance of rituals or good works:

> "But the hour is coming, and now is, when the true worshipers will worship the Father in spirit and truth; for the Father is seeking such to worship him."(John 4:23)

The scribes and Pharisees were considered by the people to be the most righteous men in the land. Because of their outward conduct, their strict adherence to the law of God as well as their great wisdom and authority, the people grew to view them as some sort of spiritual ideal. However,

Jesus proclaimed that all men are condemned by the law of God given to Moses on Mount Sinai. All men have sinned and cannot become righteous by their good works. Jesus simply echoed the words given 700 years earlier to Isaiah, declaring that the works of a man condemned him and cannot make him righteous.

> "But we are all like an unclean thing, and all our righteousnesses are like filthy rags; we all fade as a leaf, and our iniquities, like the wind, have taken us away." (Isaiah 64:6)

When Jesus taught the sermon on the mount he startled his disciples with the statement:

> "For I say to you, that unless your righteousness exceeds the righteousness of the scribes and Pharisees, you will by no means enter the kingdom of heaven." (Matthew 5:20)

This statement must have astonished the crowds that heard it. How could Jesus make such a claim? "Surely no one could be more righteous than the spiritual leaders of Israel," the people must have thought. Jesus was essentially claiming that an outward appearance of righteousness, as personified in the scribes and Pharisees, would not and could not save a man. Jesus further clarified this in stating that God is more interested in internal attitude than external performance.

> "You have heard that it was said to those of old, 'You shall not commit adultery.' But I say to you that whoever looks at a woman to lust for her has already committed adultery with her in his heart." (Matthew 5:27-28)

The righteousness of the scribes and Pharisees was a righteousness based on good works. That is, they were trying to merit God's favor by being good enough to earn eternal life. Isaiah had declared that our self attained righteousness was like filthy rags in the sight of God. The Pharisees had placed a high priority on trying to achieve a righteous standing before God by an adherence to the law. This, however, was the very same self righteousness about which Isaiah was speaking. And Jesus recognized that no man, no matter how righteous he appeared on the outside, had ever or would ever follow the law of God 100 percent.

In the verse above, Jesus expanded on this teaching of Isaiah and declared that sin could even be committed by the attitude of the heart. Therefore, an apparent outward adherence to the law could not justify a man in the sight of God. By making such a claim, Jesus was disrupting their whole tradition. This message was totally foreign to the minds that heard it. Even Jesus' disciples could hardly accept this message. The whole mind-set of the culture was that a man could be made righteous before God by attempting to follow the law of God.

Was this a message they should have expected to come from the Messiah? The answer is YES!

In chapter four we read that God would bring "a new covenant" to the people of Israel. This new covenant was necessary because the people of God had broken the previous agreement that he had given to them through Moses. God stated that this new covenant would be "written in their hearts." That is, it would involve a love relationship, through faith, rather than the works relationship of the law. And according to ancient rabbis, this "new covenant" would be brought by the Messiah.[1]

---

[1] See chapter three and the discussion on the mission of the Messiah.

This new relationship prophesied by Jeremiah was exactly what Jesus was proclaiming. A man cannot be justified (obtain a righteous standing before God) through a works relationship with God. Following a set of rules or doing good deeds just doesn't cut it. Isaiah had proclaimed this, and Jesus reaffirmed the same message.

So how can a man obtain a righteous standing before God?

A Pharisee Came by Night but Left in the Light

One evening one of the leaders of the Jews, a Pharisee, named Nicodemus came to Jesus and said:

"Rabbi, we know that You are a teacher come from God; for no one can do these signs that You do unless God is with him." (John 3:2)

Jesus responded in a most unexpected way:

"Jesus answered and said to him, 'Most assuredly, I say to you, unless one is born again, he cannot see the kingdom of God.' Nicodemus said to him, 'How can a man be born when he is old? Can he enter a second time into his mother's womb and be born?' Jesus answered, 'Most assuredly, I say to you, unless one is born of water and the Spirit, he cannot enter the kingdom of God... And as Moses lifted up the serpent in the wilderness, even so must the Son of Man be lifted up, that whoever believes in him should not perish but have eternal life. For God so loved the world that he gave his only begotten Son, that whoever believes in him should not perish but have everlasting life...He who believes in him is not condemned; but he who does not believe is condemned already, because he has not believed in the name of the only begotten Son of God.' "John 3:3-5,14-16,18)

Nicodemus, a Pharisee and a member of the Sanhedrin, was the audience for an incredible claim of Jesus. Belief in *him* would result in "everlasting life", but denying him would result in condemnation. What a radical statement! Nicodemus must have been stunned. As the ministry of Jesus developed, his claims continued to be very radical and very divisive. If Jesus was the Messiah, then a man's personal destiny depended on what one decided about him. As we shall see in the following chapters, this is only one of the many radical claims Jesus made concerning himself.

Jesus was proclaiming that a simple belief in him would give us a righteous standing before God.

We have seen in earlier chapters that, according to the Tanakh and the ancient rabbis, the Messiah speaks the very words of God himself. In Deuteronomy we saw a statement from God given to Moses:

> "I will raise up for them a Prophet like you from among their brethren, and will put My words in his mouth, and he shall speak to them all that I command him. And it shall be that whoever will not hear My words, which he speaks in My name, I will require it of him." (Deuteronomy 18:18-19)

So, according to God himself, we had better heed the words of the Messiah. If Jesus is the Messiah, then it is critical that we take his teaching seriously.

More Unexpected Messages

> "But I say to you, love your enemies, bless those who curse you, do good to those who hate you, and pray for those who spitefully use you and persecute you." (Matthew 5:44)

Jesus of Nazareth was a simple man with no place to call home. To his disciples, he proclaimed that the poor, the meek, the hungry, the thirsty, the merciful, the pure in heart, the peacemakers and those persecuted for his name's sake would inherit the kingdom of God.[1]

When his disciples expected Jesus to condemn someone, he would love them. When they expected him to honor and respect someone, such as the Pharisees, he would often rebuke them. He taught that they should pray for those who had abused them. He said that they should love their enemies and forgive an offense seventy times seven times! He said they should pay taxes to Caesar, and if compelled to carry a Roman soldier's pack one mile, to go two. He simply did not meet the Messianic mold they had expected.

The disciples must have thought to themselves, "Where is the powerful military leader? When will Jesus blow away the Romans and set up his kingdom? Why is Jesus so harsh with the leaders, those righteous men of the Sanhedrin?"

I believe it was the tremendous gap between what they expected in the Messiah and what they saw in the message, ministry and destiny of this carpenter from Nazareth, that led the majority of the people (including the leadership) to reject him.

Was the Paradox Expected?

"Do you suppose that I came to give peace on earth?
I tell you, not at all, but rather division"
Jesus of Nazareth (Luke 12:51)

---

[1]Matthew . 5:1-12.

Jesus was acutely aware that his life, claims and ministry created tremendous division in the nation of Israel as well as in the families of his followers. This tension is something that almost every follower of Jesus experiences on an almost daily basis. Families often become divided when one member converts to Christianity and tries to evangelize the others. For the Jewish believer in Jesus, conversion can even mean the loss of the entire family.

If Jesus of Nazareth is the Messiah, the paradoxical reaction of the crowds toward him must be explained. It is very difficult for the modern Jewish person to believe that the Messiah could engender such wide ranging and almost irreconcilable reactions at the same time. How can this be? It is clear that if the Messianic claims of Jesus are to stand then this dichotomy must be evaluated in the light of biblical expectations. Was this paradoxical reaction toward the Messiah prophesied to occur in the Tanakh?

The answer is YES! The Messiah was vividly predicted to cause such a division.

As we saw in our examination of the suffering servant, the Messiah would be despised and rejected, and yet would be exalted by God and rule the people on David's throne. It is fascinating to note that just such a paradoxical reaction was anticipated by the prophet Isaiah.

"Behold, My Servant shall prosper, he shall be exalted and lifted up and be very high." (Isaiah 52:13, JPS, 1917)

Yet, the prophet continues:

"He is despised and forsaken of men, a man of sorrows and acquainted with grief. And as one from whom men hide their face: He was despised, and we did esteem

him not...Therefore, I will divide him a portion among the great, and he shall divide the spoil with the mighty, because he bared his soul unto death, and was numbered with the transgressors; Yet he bore the sin of many, and made intercession for the transgressors."
(Isaiah 53:3,12, JPS, 1917)

The paradoxical reactions to the Messiah are here clearly proclaimed, side by side, by the prophet Isaiah. The literal Hebrew rendering of this verse is that he is to be lifted up (exalted), magnified, and be exceedingly lofty (and be very high).

Now for the rabbi who might argue that there are two individuals spoken of here, I would point out that the subject of the text is spoken of in the singular personal pronoun only! There is no textual indication that there are multiple individuals spoken of here.

This Messianic prophecy predicted over 700 years before the birth of Jesus that the Messiah would inspire both exaltation and revulsion at the same time!

In Psalm 22, viewed by early rabbis as a Messianic passage, we see the same reaction to the subject of this scripture.

"But I am a worm, and no man; A reproach of men, and despised of the people...The poor shall eat and be satisfied; Those who seek him will praise the LORD. Let your heart live forever!...All the prosperous of the earth Shall eat and worship; All those who go down to the dust Shall bow before him, Even he who cannot keep himself alive...A posterity shall serve him. It will be recounted of the Lord to the next generation...They will come and declare his righteousness to a people who will be born, That he has done this." (Psalm 22:6,26,29,30,31)

Again we see the themes of rejection and praise in the same section of scripture. Once more, only singular personal pronouns are used, meaning that both these characteristics must apply to the same person.

The Stone of Stumbling and Rock of Offense

The paradoxical reaction to the Messiah is again pointed out in a very provocative scripture found in Isaiah. Speaking of the Messiah, Isaiah states:

"He will be for a sanctuary, but for a stone of stumbling and for a rock of offense to both the houses of Israel, as a gin (a trap) and a snare to the inhabitants of Jerusalem" (Isaiah 8:14, JPS , 1917)[1]

This fascinating scripture predicted that when the Messiah came he would "stumble" and "offend" both houses of Israel.[2] And yet, he would be as a sanctuary to some of the people.

The word translated "stone of stumbling" implies that Israel would be perplexed and make a misstep regarding the Messiah. Clearly, the nation and leadership were perplexed by the carpenter from Nazareth. And if he is the Messiah, then his rejection by the leadership of Israel was a misstep, a stumbling of monumental proportions.

Chief Cornerstone Rejected

One of the most beautiful portions of scripture in the Bible is Psalm 118. The psalmist spends the first portion of

---

[1]This was specifically applied to the Messiah in the Babylonian Talmud, Shebhuoth 35b.

[2]That is the northern kingdom of Israel and the southern kingdom of Judah.

the chapter praising God for his mercy, his refuge and his salvation. Then in the middle of the Psalm we find an unexpected declaration about "the stone which the builders rejected."

"I will give thanks unto Thee, for thou hast answered me, and art become my salvation. The stone which the builders rejected is become the chief corner-stone. This is the Lord's doing; It is marvelous in our eyes." (Psalm 118:21-23, JPS, 1917)

In the midst of praising the Lord, the psalmist declares that "the stone" that is rejected later becomes "the chief corner-stone." According to the Psalm, this contradictory reaction to the "stone" will eventually be viewed by the people as "marvelous in our eyes." Could it be that this is a veiled prophecy of the initial rejection and ultimate recognition of the Messiah?

According to Jesus this is exactly what the psalmist was declaring. He applied this prophecy to himself after a parable in which he predicted his rejection by the leadership.[1]

As we will see, the rejection of the Messiah was part of a plan of God that will ultimately be viewed by the people as "marvelous in our eyes."

The Carpenter's Credentials

In the life and ministry of Jesus we have a paradoxical composite. The New Testament declares he was born of a virgin in the city of Bethlehem, from the line of David. Through his ministry he brought a new covenant to Israel. He has been worshipped by billions as the Messiah, yet

---

[1]Luke 20:17.

because of his radical claims, has been a stumbling block to the nation of Israel. He was despised by the leadership and rejected, just as Isaiah had foretold.

Ultimately, Jesus was crucified by the Romans, but (according to the New Testament documents) he rose from the dead on the third day. A hoax? A fairy tale? We will examine these questions later.

Keep an open mind as we push forward through some astonishing ancient rabbinical beliefs, as well as powerful new evidence from the Dead Sea Scrolls. This evidence will further reveal the true nature, mission and identity of the Messiah.

CHAPTER 5

MESSIAH–THE SON OF GOD?

" 'I will declare the decree:' The LORD has said to
Me, 'You are My Son, Today I have begotten You.' "
(Psalm 2:7)

One of the most contentious issues between modern
day Jewish and Christian scholars is whether the Messiah
would be the "Son of God." The Christian New Testament
clearly indicates that Jesus believed he was the Son of God,
and that the disciples believed this as well. However, most
twentieth century rabbis claim that the Messiah is simply a
man.

In 1992 I had a discussion about the Messiah with a
Jewish physician, a man who was a Torah scholar as well.
He told me that virtually all modern rabbis believe the
Messiah is going to be just a man. He will be great in
wisdom and stature, but he will be just a man. He will not
be the Son of God, nor will he be God in the flesh. He then
went on to tell me that the belief that the Messiah is the
Son of God was a Christian fabrication. He told me that
there is no evidence from the Old Testament or the writings
of the ancient rabbis that the Messiah would be the Son of
God. Even today, when one asks a modern rabbi why he
rejects the Messiahship of Jesus, he will often say,
"Because Jesus claimed to be the Son of God!"

This denial among virtually all of modern Judaism of the
"Sonship" of the Messiah is widely held. However, this has

not always been so. There is abundant evidence in the writings of the ancient rabbis, as well as the Apocryphal books, that the Messiah would indeed be the Son of God.

In 1992, powerful new evidence from the Dead Sea Scrolls was published that reveals the belief among first century mainstream Judaism that the Messiah was indeed the Son of God. Before we look at that evidence, let's look at the claims of Jesus, his disciples and the leaders of the Jewish nation who rejected him as their Messiah.

Jesus: Son of God or Son of Beelzebub?[1]

When Jesus of Nazareth was arrested by the Sanhedrin, he was accused of blasphemy.[2] What was it that he said that made them accuse him of that? He claimed to be the Son of God.

While in heated debate with the religious leaders of his day, Jesus stated:

> "Do you say of him whom the Father sanctified and sent into the world, 'You are blaspheming,' because I said, 'I am the Son of God?' " (John 10:36)

After Jesus had healed a blind man, that man was questioned by the leaders of the Jews as to who was responsible. The man said he did not know who had healed him. Later, when Jesus found him alone, we find this interesting discourse:

---

[1]Beelzebub is an ancient name for Satan.
[2]Blasphemy in this case was claiming to be God or claiming equality with him.

"Jesus heard that they had cast him out; and when he had found him, he said to him, 'Do you believe in the Son of God?' He answered and said, 'Who is he, Lord, that I may believe in him?' And Jesus said to him, 'You have both seen him and it is he who is talking with you.' " (John 9:35-36)

When Peter, a Jewish fisherman and one of Jesus' disciples, was asked by Jesus, "who do you say that I am?", Peter responded:

"You are the Christ, the Son of the living God.
(Matthew 16:16)

Another disciple, John, wrote of Jesus in his gospel:

" I have seen and testified that this is the Son of God."
(John 1:49)

While under arrest, Jesus admits to the Sanhedrin that he was the Son of God. They immediately took him to Pontius Pilate where they accused him of claiming to be the Christ (Messiah in Greek), a king.

"Then they all said, 'Are You then the Son of God?' And he said to them, 'You rightly say that I am.' And they said, 'What further testimony do we need? For we have heard it ourselves from his own mouth.' Then the whole multitude of them arose and led him to Pilate. And they began to accuse him, saying, 'We found this fellow perverting the nation, and forbidding to pay taxes to Caesar, saying that he himself is Christ, a King.' So Pilate asked him, saying, 'Are You the King of the Jews?' And he answered him and said, 'It is as you say.' " (Luke 22:70-23:3)

What is fascinating about this discourse is that the members of the Sanhedrin equated the claim of being "the Son of God" with claiming to be the Christ!–the Messiah!

In another passage we see that the Pharisees told Pontius Pilate that the reason they wanted him tried was because Jesus claimed to be the Son of God (a title they associated with the Messiah).

> "The Jews answered him, 'We have a law, and according to our law he ought to die, because he made himself the Son of God.' " (John 19:7)

The point is obvious. Jesus said he was the Son of God, the disciples claimed he was the Son of God and the Pharisees took him to Pilate to be tried for claiming to be the Son of God.

Now the skeptic might say that this doesn't prove that ancient rabbis believed that the Messiah would be the Son of God. But an examination of early rabbinic literature bolsters this conclusion.

Psalm 2 "You Are My Son"

In the book of Psalms, chapter two, we have a provocative scripture where God speaks of his anointed servant, and someone whom he calls *"my Son."*

> "Why do the nations rage and the people plot a vain thing? The kings of the earth set themselves, and the rulers take counsel together, **against the LORD and against his anointed,** saying, 'let us break their bonds in pieces and cast away their cords from us.' He who sits in the heavens shall laugh; the Lord shall hold them in derision. Then he shall speak to them in his wrath, and distress them in his deep displeasure: 'Yet I

have set My King on my holy hill of Zion.' `I will declare the decree the Lord has said to me, **you are my Son, today I have begotten you.** Ask of me and I will give you the nations for your inheritance, and the ends of the earth for your possession.' "

In this prophecy we see a reference to the LORD, (יהוה) (YAHWEH–one of the names of God) and his anointed, מׁשׁיח (Hebrew for Messiah). The LORD states to this Anointed One, "**You are my Son, today I have begotten you.**" To this Anointed One, the Lord God of Israel will give the nations for his inheritance! Who is this "anointed one?" The word מׁשׁיח is the word Mashiyach or Messiah and is translated as "anointed."

Most modern rabbis, however, declare that this is not *"The Messiah."* They claim that this is an anointed one, one of many, but not the Messiah of Israel.

However, when we examine the ancient rabbinical literature on this Psalm, we find that it is applied to the Messiah in numerous places in the Talmud,[1] and even in medieval Midrashic rabbinical sources. [2]

In chapter two we saw a fascinating quote in the Midrash which ties the sufferings of the servant in Isaiah 53 with the "Anointed One" in Psalm 2:

"Rabbi in the name of Rabbi Acha says: 'The sufferings are divided into three parts: one for David and the fathers, one for our own generation, and one for the King Messiah, and this is what is written, "He was wounded for our transgressions," etc. "And when the hour comes," says the Holy One, blessed be he, to

---

[1]Babylonian Talmud, tractate Sukkah 52a.
[2]Midrash on Psalm 2, Psalm 92:11, 1 Samuel 16:1, Genesis 44.

them: "I must create him *1* a new creation, as even it is said, 'This day have I begotten you.' "*2,3*

So here we see that the Messiah would suffer for our transgressions and afterwards he would be created as a new creature! The writer of this remarkable passage recognized that the suffering servant of Isaiah 53 (*he was wounded for our transgressions*) and the "Anointed One" in Psalm 2 (*This day I have begotten you*) were indeed the same individual!

In the Yakult Shemoni, there is a rather provocative commentary regarding the second verse in Psalm 2 .

" 'Against God , and his Messiah,' likening them[4] to a robber who stands defiantly behind the palace of the King and says, '**If I shall find the son of the King, I shall lay hold of him, and crucify him, and kill him with cruel death.**' But the Holy Spirit mocks at him, 'He that sits in the heavens laughs, Jehovah has them in derision.' "[5]

The writer of this fascinating commentary declares that the gentile nations will "crucify the Son of the King." The King in Psalm two is God and the "Son of the King" in this context is a clear reference to the Messiah. This observation comes from a rabbi in the middle ages!

In the Babylonian Talmud there is another fascinating discussion about the second Psalm. The writer of this portion of the Talmud quotes multiple passages from Psalm 2 and goes on to apply them as specifically referring to the

---

[1]The Messiah.
[2] Midrash Tellihim on Psalm 2 and Midrash Samuel chapter 19.
[3]For a detailed discussion of Psalm 2 see *The Life and Times of Jesus the Messiah,* Alfred Edersheim, Appendix IX, pg. 716-717.
[4]The gentile nations.
[5]Yakult Shemoni, (vol. 2 par. 620, pg. 90a) .See Edersheim, Vol. 2, pg. 716.

Messiah. In this section of the Talmud, the rabbis ask the question:

> "But when the battle of Gog and Magog will come about they will be asked, 'For what purpose have you come?' And they will reply: '**Against God and his Messiah**' as it is said, '**why are the nations in an uproar and why do the people mutter in vain,**' as it is said, '**let us break their bands asunder, and the holy one blessed be he will sit and laugh**' as it is said: '**he that sitteth in heaven laughs...**' "

This remarkable quotation from the Talmud, we read the rabbis specifically quoting from Psalm 2 and applying it to the battle of Gog and Magog, an end time battle. The writer of this portion specifically applies this to God and his Messiah![1]

"Son of God" in the Book of Enoch

In the book of Enoch, one of the Apocryphal books[2] dated 170-130 B.C.E., contains much discussion about the Messiah. There are several terms given as specific designations of the Messiah. In chapter 62:5 the Messiah is referred to as "the woman's Son." In chapter 48:2 the Messiah is referred to as "the Son of Man, the Elect and the Just One." And the Messiah is expressly designated in the oldest portion of the book as "the Son of God" (105:2). So we can see that the reference to the Messiah being the Son of God was not an unknown concept around the time of Jesus of Nazareth.

---

[1]Babylonian Talmud Abodah Zarah 3b.

[2]Apocryphal books are books written usually by unknown Jewish authorities between the completion of the Tanakh and the writing of the New Testament. These books are not accepted as part of the canon of scripture by most Jewish or Christian sources.

"Son of God" in the Dead Sea Scrolls

The discovery and translation of the Dead Sea Scrolls has been a tremendous boost to our understanding of the beliefs and culture of the Jewish people during the first century C.E.

In the fall of 1991 the remaining unpublished portions of the Dead Sea Scrolls were released to libraries around the world. A number of new fragments have come forth which have provided remarkable new insights regarding the Messianic beliefs of the Qumran Jews during that period.

The people of the Qumran community, the apparent writers of the scrolls, have been described as "religious end time zealots" by some scholars, and as mainstream Jews by others. One thing is certain, they wrote extensively about the Messiah. Therefore, if the Messiah was believed to be the Son of God by ancient Jews, then it should not be surprising to find that belief expressed in the writings of the Dead Sea Scrolls. In fact, that is exactly what we find.

The "Son of God" Fragment 4Q246

A portion of the Dead Sea Scrolls, called the "Son of God" fragment 4Q246,[1] we see an astonishing reference to a supernatural Messiah who is called the Son of God:

> "He shall be called the Son of the God; they will call him the Son of the Most High...He will judge the earth in righteousness...and every nation will bow down to

---

[1]This means it was found in cave 4 of the Qumran community (Q) and is catalogued as fragment 246.

him…with (God's) help he will make war, and…[God] will give all the peoples into his power."[1]

The passage is filled with undeniable Messianic images. The writer of this text believed that the Messiah would "judge the earth in righteousness" and that the nations "will bow down to him." The text speaks not of multiple Messiah figures but of a *single* individual. This Messiah figure is triumphant and exalted and specifically referred to as the "Son of God…Son of the Most High!" His strength, accomplishments and character clearly reveal that he is not an ordinary man, but he was believed by these people to be a supernatural being.

To find a Messianic figure being called "the Son of God," the "Son of the Most High," by the Jewish believers in Qumran is astonishing and conclusive! To them, the Messiah would be the Son of God!

In another recently published Dead Sea Scroll text, fragment 4Q521, we find another reference to a single Messiah figure who also possesses supernatural "god–like" traits. It describes the resurrection of the dead occurring as a result of the Messiah's work and contains language which parallels the New Testament Gospels of Matthew and Luke.

The 4Q521 text reads as follows:

"The heavens and the earth will obey his Messiah, the sea and all that is in them. He will not turn aside from the commandment of the Holy Ones. Take strength in his mighty work all ye who seek the Lord. Will ye not find the Lord in this, all ye who wait for him with hope in your hearts? Surely the Lord will seek out the

---

[1]*Biblical Archaeology Review;* November/December 1992, Michael Wise and James Tabor.

pious, and will call the righteous by name. His spirit will hover over the poor; by his might will he restore the faithful. He will glorify the pious on the throne of the eternal kingdom. **He will release the captives, make the blind see, raise up the down trodden.** Forever I will cleave to him against the powerful and I will trust in his loving kindness and in his goodness forever. His holy Messiah will not be slow in coming. **And as for the wonders that are not the work of the Lord, when he, that is the Messiah, comes then he will heal the sick, resurrect the dead, and to the poor announce glad tidings.** He will lead the holy ones, he will shepherd them. He will do all of it."

In this fascinating text we see a remarkable similarity to the beliefs of Orthodox Christianity regarding the Messiah. The Jews at Qumran believed that the Messiah would be the Son of God, that he would be a supernatural being, that he would raise the dead, heal the sick and announce glad tidings to the poor. Clearly no ordinary man could do such work. These two scroll fragments are believed by scholars to be as old as 100 B.C.E.!

Most modern rabbis and Jewish Bible scholars claim that the belief that the Messiah would be a supernatural Son of God is a Christian doctrine and not a rabbinical one. Clearly, however, the evidence from the Talmud and the Dead Sea Scrolls now nullifies that allegation. The Christian Messianic beliefs regarding the "Sonship" and supernatural character of the Messiah are doctrines that were espoused by the Jews at Qumran as well as the Hebrew sages. The evidence speaks for itself. According to the views of ancient Judaism, the Messiah is the Son of God!

CHAPTER 6

THE TIME OF MESSIAH'S COMING

One of the most interesting aspects of rabbinic Messianic speculation has to do with the time of his coming. Following the Babylonian captivity, which was from 606- 537 B.C.E., the rabbis began to pore through the Scriptures to find clues regarding the time of Messiah's coming. As we shall see, there were many prophecies which they believed were specific indicators of the time when Messiah would be expected.

Some have stated that there have always been intense Messianic expectations throughout the ages, and that those expectations were no different during the time period of the ministry of Jesus of Nazareth. However, a study of such expectations reveals this is not the case. During the first two quarters of the first century C.E., more than at any time in history, Messianic expectations were very high. Why was this so?

Was this great Messianic expectation at the time of Jesus simply because the Jews were suffering severely under the Roman yoke? Or was it because Bible prophecy pointed to that period of time as the time of Israel's appointment with Messiah?

In the book by Rabbi Abba Hillel Silver, *A History of Messianic Speculation in Israel*, we read about the tremendous expectations at the time of Jesus Christ that the Messiah would come soon. The reasons for this hope are explained in the following quotes:

> "Prior to the first century (C.E.) the Messianic interest was not excessive...The First Century, however, especially the generation before the destruction [of the Second Temple] witnessed a remarkable outburst of Messianic emotionalism. This is to be attributed, as we shall see, not to an intensification of Roman persecution, but to the prevalent belief induced by the popular chronology of that day that the age was on the threshold of the Millennium...When Jesus came into Galilee, 'spreading the gospel of the Kingdom of God,' and saying the 'time is fulfilled' and the Kingdom of God is at hand,' he was voicing the opinion universally held that...the age of the Kingdom of God-was at hand...It was this chronological fact which inflamed the Messianic hope rather than the Roman persecutions...**Jesus appeared in the procuratorship of Pontius Pilate (26-36 C.E.)**...It seems likely, therefore, that in the minds of the people the Millennium was to begin around the year 30 C.E. Be it remembered that it is not the Messiah who brings about the Millennium. It is the inevitable advent of the Millennium which carries along with it the Messiah and his appointed activities. **The Messiah was expected around the second quarter of the First Century C.E. because the Millennium was at hand. Prior to that time he was not expected, because according to the**

chronology of the day the Millennium was still considerably removed."[1]

Rabbi Silver makes several remarkable points. First, the Messiah was not expected prior to the first century "because of the chronology of the day." As we will see, there were chronological indicators, recognized as such by the rabbis, which pinpointed the time period, even the very day that the Messiah would come.

Secondly, it was this understanding of biblical chronology and prophecy, rather than the suffering of the people, that led to the tremendous expectation that the Messiah was soon to come.

The Desire of All Nations

In the book of Haggai we find an interesting prophecy that indicates that the Messiah would come to the Second Temple. Haggai prophesied in the years 520-516 B.C.E. At that time, the Jews had been back in the land for a generation; however, the city of Jerusalem and the Second Temple had not yet been completely rebuilt. Yet, Haggai prophesied that the "Desire of All Nations" (an idiom for the Messiah) would come to the Second Temple.

"For thus says the LORD of hosts: 'Once more, **it is a little while**, I will shake heaven and earth, the sea and dry land; and I will shake all nations, and they shall come to **the Desire of All Nations**, and I will fill **this** temple with glory,' says the LORD of hosts. 'The silver is Mine, and the gold is Mine,' says the LORD of hosts.' The **glory of this latter temple shall be greater than the former**,' says the LORD of hosts. 'And in this place I will give peace,' says the LORD of hosts." (Haggai 2:6-9)

---

[1] *A History of Messianic Speculation in Israel,* Rabbi Abba Hillel Silver, 1927, Macmillan Co. ,pg. 5-7, ISBN 0-8446-2937-5

This portion of scripture makes several specific predictions.

1. The LORD is going to shake heaven and earth.

2. All the nations will come to The "Desire of All Nations", an idiom for the Messiah.

3. God would fill "this temple," i.e. the Second Temple with glory.

4. The glory of the Second Temple would be greater than the first.

5. Finally, notice the emphasis on the timing; "It is a little while."

This prophecy is specifically applied to the time of the coming of the Messiah in the Midrash.[1]

To the Jewish mind, the coming of the Messiah is believed to be an event that truly will "shake the heavens and the earth." This will be the event that will restore the nation of Israel to the place of prominence that it once enjoyed under the reign of King David. The Messiah (here referred to as "the Desire of All Nations") will be sought, not only by the nation of Israel, but by the gentile nations as well.

The prophet states that God would fill "This Temple" with glory. Which Temple? The obvious answer is that Haggai was referring to the one that stood during his day or possibly a future temple. We can tell this by the context of the passage. He states that the glory of this latter temple, would exceed that of the first.

---

[1] Tractate Debharim Rabba, (Midrash on Deuteronomy) 1, ed Warsh, pg 4b line 15 from the top.

Now we know that from an architectural point of view the Second Temple was not nearly as impressive as the First Temple built by King Solomon. Nevertheless, God said that he would fill the Second Temple with his glory and that its glory would exceed that of the First Temple. Therefore, since it did not exceed the first from a material, architectural point of view, the prophet must be speaking of another type of glory.

During the days of the First Temple we know that the glory of God filled the Holy of Holies. However, before its destruction, the Shekinah glory of God left the Holy of Holies of that temple. When the Second Temple was built, including the Holy of Holies, there is no record in the Bible that the Shekinah glory of God ever dwelt in that temple.

So how could the glory of God fill the Second Temple to the point of exceeding the glory of the first? One way would be for the "Desire of All Nations," the Messiah of Israel, to come to and teach in that Second Temple!

The rabbis believed that the glory of God dwelt in the Messiah. Therefore, his appearance in the Second Temple would certainly qualify as an event that would cause the "glory of the latter temple to exceed the first." However, the Second Temple was destroyed by the Romans in the year 70 C.E. Therefore, if the glory of the Second Temple was to exceed the first, some glorious event, an event of biblical proportions, had to occur in the Second Temple before its destruction in 70 C.E. If we search the Tanakh and the writings of the ancient rabbis, we are unable to find the event that could fulfill this prophecy. Did the prophet mess up?

During his life, Jesus of Nazareth taught in the Second Temple. The first time was at the age of twelve. Jesus even prophesied its destruction in Luke 19:43-45:

"For the days will come upon you when your enemies
will build an embankment around you, surround you
and close you in on every side, and level you, and your
children within you, to the ground; and they will not
leave in you one stone upon another, because you did
not know the time of your visitation."

Surely the life, ministry, teachings and bodily
resurrection of Jesus of Nazareth have shaken the
foundations of the earth. Many peoples have come to the
"Desire of All Nations" and his presence in the Second
Temple certainly caused the glory of that temple to exceed
the glory of the first!

The First Temple was limited to a faint whisper of
God's presence, a spiritual manifestation of the creator.
But, if Jesus is who he claimed, then in him we had both the
physical and spiritual manifestation of the Almighty
Creator of the universe, Jesus, the God–Man, who walked
and taught in the temple. Surely, the glory of the Second
Temple exceeded the first!

Until Shiloh Comes

In Genesis, chapter 49, we read of the last blessing that
Jacob bestowed to his sons.

"And Jacob called his sons and said, 'Gather together,
that I may tell you what shall befall you in the last
days.' " (Genesis 49:1)

When he had gathered them together he began to
prophesy over each of them. When he finally got to his son
Judah he gave a prophecy concerning the Messiah.

"The scepter shall not depart from Judah, nor a
lawgiver from between his feet, until Shiloh comes;

and to him shall be the obedience of the people."
(Genesis 49:10)

This strange prophecy has several words that need to
be defined in order to be fully understood. The "scepter"
has been understood to mean the "tribal staff" or "tribal
identity." This "tribal identity" was linked, in the minds of
the Jews, to their right to apply and enforce Mosaic law
upon the people, including the right to adjudicate capital
cases and administer capital punishment, or *jus gladii*. [1] As
we shall see, there is abundant evidence from the writings
from the ancient rabbis that the name "Shiloh" is an idiom
for the Messiah.

Therefore, according to this prophecy, the tribal
identity or scepter of the tribe of Judah would not cease
until the Messiah came. Judah was not only the name of the
son of Jacob, but it was also the name of the southern
kingdom of the divided nation of Israel.

With these definitions in place we can restate the
prophecy as follows:

"The [national identity of Judah, which includes the
right to enforce Mosaic law, including the right to
administer capital punishment upon the people, as called
for in the Torah] shall not depart from [the southern
kingdom (Judah)], nor a lawgiver from between his feet,
until Shiloh [the Messiah] comes; and to him shall be the
obedience of the people."

This prophecy gives specific indicators regarding the
time of the coming of the Messiah. The prophecy declares
that he would come before the right to impose Jewish law

---

[1] *jus gladii* means the authority to adjudicate capital cases and impose
capital punishment.

(which includes capital punishment) is rescinded and before the national identity of Judah was removed.

During the seventy-year Babylonian captivity, from 606-537 B.C.E., the southern kingdom of Israel, Judah, had lost its national sovereignty, but it retained its tribal staff or national identity.[1] It is very significant that in the book of Ezra we read that during the seventy-year Babylonian captivity, the Jews still retained their own lawgivers or judges.[2] They maintained their identity and judicial authority over their own people even during seventy years of slavery. The scepter had not been lost during the Babylonian captivity.

During the next five centuries the Jews suffered under the rulership of the Medo-Persian, Greek and Roman Empires. Yet, Judah retained its tribal identity up until the first quarter of the first century C.E.

In the first quarter of the first century C.E. the Jews were under Roman dominion when an unprecedented event occurred. According to Josephus (Antiquities 17:13) around the year 6-7 C.E., the son and successor to King Herod, a man named Herod Archelaus, was dethroned and banished to Vienna, a city of Gaul.[3] He was replaced, not by a Jewish king, but by a Roman procurator named Caponius.

---

[1] Paraphrased from *Evidence That Demands a Verdict*, Josh McDowell, Here's Life Publishers, pg. 168.

[2] See Ezra 1:5,8 where we read of the priests and prince of Judah, still in existence after seventy years away from Israel.

[3] Archelaus was the second son of Herod the Great. Herod's oldest son, Herod Antipater, was murdered by Herod the Great, along with a number of other family members. Archelaus' mother was a Samaritan, giving him only one quarter, or less, Jewish blood. At the death of Herod the Great in 4 B.C.E, Archelaus was placed over Judea as "Entharch" by Caesar Augustus. However, he was never accepted by the Jews and was removed from office in 6 or 7 C.E.

The legal power of the Sanhedrin was immediately restricted.

With the ascension of Caponius the Sanhedrin lost their ability to adjudicate capital cases. This was the normal policy toward all the nations under the yoke of the Romans. The province of Judea had been spared from this policy up to this point, however, Caesar Agustus had had enough of the Jews and finally removed the judicial authority from them at the ascension of Caponius. This transfer of power was recorded by Josephus.[1]

> "And now Archelaus' part of Judea was reduced into a province, and Caponius, one of the equestrian order of the Romans, was sent as a procurator, **having the power of life and death put into his hands by Caesar!**"

The power of the Sanhedrin to adjudicate capital cases was immediately removed. In the minds of the Jewish leadership, this event signified the removal of the scepter or national identity of the tribe of Judah!

If you think that this is a Christian contrivance, think again. Here are several ancient rabbinical references that indicate that the rabbis believed that Genesis 49:10 was referring to the Messiah.

In the Targum Onkelos it states:

> "The transmission of dominion shall not cease from the house of Judah, nor the scribe from his children's children, forever, **until Messiah comes.**" [2]

---

[1] *Wars of the Jews*, Book 2, chapter 8.
[2] *The Messiah: An Aramaic Interpretation; The Messianic Exegesis of the Targum*, Samson H. Levy (Cincinnati: Hebrew Union College Jewish Institute of Religion, 1974), pg. 2.

The Targum Pseudo-Jonathan states:

"Kings and rulers shall not cease from the house of
Judah...until King Messiah comes" [1]

And Targum Yerushalmi states:

"Kings shall not cease from the house of Judah...**until
the time of the coming of the King Messiah...to**
whom all the dominions of the earth shall become
subservient." [2]

In the Babylonian Talmud, Sanhedrin 98b, Rabbi
Johanan said:

"The world was created for the sake of the Messiah,
what is this Messiah's name? **The school of Rabbi
Shila said 'his name is Shiloh, for it is written;
until Shiloh come.'** "

These amazing commentaries should eliminate any
doubt that the Jews who lived prior to the Christian era
believed that one of the names of the Messiah was Shiloh.
Furthermore, these quotes should eliminate all doubt that
the ancient rabbis believed the Messiah would come before
the removal of the scepter from Judah.

Woe Unto Us, For
Messiah Has Not Appeared!

So far we have established that Shiloh is an idiom for
the Messiah and that the scepter (that is, the tribal identity,

---

[1] i*The Messiah: An Aramaic Interpretation; The Messianic Exegesis of the
Targum*, Samson H. Levy (Cincinnati: Hebrew Union College Jewish
Institute of Religion, 1974), pg. 7
[2] ibid., pg. 8

associated with the right to impose capital punishment) had departed from the kingdom of Judah, early in the first quarter of the first century. What was the reaction of the Jews when the right to adjudicate capital cases (*jus gladii*) was removed from Judah? Did they view the removal of their authority on capital cases as the removal of the scepter from Judah? The answer can categorically be stated as YES!

When Archelaus was banished, the power of the Sanhedrin was severely curtailed. Capital cases could no longer be tried by the Sanhedrin. Such cases were now transferred to the Roman procurator, Caponius. This transfer of power is even mentioned in the Talmud:

"A little more than forty years before the destruction of the Temple, the power of pronouncing capital sentences was taken away from the Jews." [1]

This certainly corresponds to the same event recorded by Josephus we saw earlier. In Antiquities 20:9 Josephus again points out that the Sanhedrin had no authority over capital cases:

"After the death of the procurator Festus, when Albinus was about to succeed him, the high-priest Ananius considered it a favorable opportunity to assemble the Sanhedrin. He therefore caused James the brother of Jesus, who was called Christ, and several others, to appear before this hastily assembled council, and pronounced upon them the sentence of death by stoning. All the wise men and strict observers of the law who were at Jerusalem expressed their disapprobation of this act...Some even went to Albinus himself, who had departed to Alexandria, to bring this breach of the law under his observation, and to inform him that Ananius had acted illegally in

---

[1] Jerusalem Talmud, Sanhedrin, folio 24.

assembling the Sanhedrin without the Roman authority."

This remarkable passage not only mentions Jesus of Nazareth and his brother James as historical figures, but it also declares that the Sanhedrin had no authority to pass the death sentence upon any man!

The *jus gladii*, the right to impose the death sentence, had been removed. The remaining authority of Judah had been taken away by the Romans in the early years of the first century. The scepter had departed from Judah. Its royal and legal powers were removed; but where was Shiloh?

The reaction of the Jews to these monumental events is recorded in the Talmud. Augustin Lemann in his book *Jesus Before the Sanhedrin* records a statement by Rabbi Rachmon:

"When the members of the Sanhedrin found themselves deprived of their right over life and death, a general consternation took possession of them: they covered their heads with ashes, and their bodies with sackcloth, exclaiming: **'Woe unto us for the scepter has departed from Judah and the Messiah has not come.'**"[1,2,3]

---

[1] Babylonian Talmud, Chapter 4, folio 37.
[2] *Jesus Before the Sanhedrin*, by Augustin Lemann, 1886, Translated by Julius Magath, NL# 0239683, Library of Congress # 15-24973
[3] See also the monumental work *Pugio Fidei*, Martini, Raymundus, published by De Vosin in 1651. For a detailed discussion of this reference see *The Fifty Third Chapter of Isaiah According to Jewish Interpreters*, preface pg. iv S.R. Driver, A.D. Neubauer, KTAV Publishing House, Inc. New York, 1969.

The scepter was smitten from the hands of the tribe of Judah, while the kingdom of Judea, the last remnant of the greatness of Israel, was debased into being merely a part of the province of Syria. While the Jews wept in the streets of Jerusalem, there was growing up in the city of Nazareth the young son of a Jewish carpenter, Jesus of Nazareth. The inescapable conclusion was that **Shiloh had come–Only then was the scepter removed!**

Daniel's Prophecy of the Seventy Weeks

In a city called Babylon around the year 537 B.C.E., a Hebrew named Daniel, while deep in prayer, was interrupted by an angel named Gabriel. Daniel had been praying for the people of Israel when the angel stated that he had come to give Daniel "skill and understanding" regarding the future of the nation.

In the book of Daniel 9:24-26 we find the angel's statement.

"Seventy sevens are determined for your people and for your holy city, to finish the transgression, to make an end of sins, to make reconciliation for iniquity, to bring in everlasting righteousness, to seal up vision and prophecy and to anoint the most holy. Know therefore and understand, that from the going forth of the command to restore and rebuild Jerusalem until Messiah the Prince, there shall be seven sevens and sixty two sevens; the street shall be built again, and the wall, even in troublesome times. And after the sixty two sevens the Messiah shall be cut off, but not for himself; and the people of the prince who is to come shall destroy the city and the sanctuary." (Daniel 9:24-26)

This message pinpointed the time of the coming of the long awaited "Messiah the Prince" (מָשִׁיחַ נָגִיד).

At the time of this angelic visitation, Jerusalem was completely desolate. The majority of Israelites had been taken captive by the Babylonians. The city of Jerusalem (including the Temple) had been destroyed by the Babylonian empire 70 years earlier. The Hebrew people were, however, about to be freed by the Medo-Persian king Cyrus.

The prophecy states that "seventy sevens" are determined for the people of Israel. In Hebrew the word translated as "sevens" is the plural form of the word "shabua" (שָׁבוּעַ), which literally means a week of years; much like the English word decade means ten years.

The prophecy declares that Daniel should "know and understand" that from the going forth of the command to restore and rebuild Jerusalem, until the Messiah the Prince comes, that there will be sixty two sevens and seven sevens of years. Therefore, if a seven (shabua) is seven years, then 69 sevens is 483 years (69 x 7= 483 years). Some scholars believe that at that time in history most of the known ancient calendars calculated a year as 360 days (Chinese, Mayan, Egyptian, Hebrew, Babylonian and many others).[1] Some scholars believe an astronomical event (e.g., a close passing of Mars, a meteor or comet striking the earth) lengthened the time the earth takes to rotate one time around the sun to the current 365.25 days per year.[2] Scholars also believe that for prophetic calendars the Jews used a 360 day calendar year.

---

[1] See *Footprints of the Messiah*, Chuck Missler, Koinonia House, PO Box D, Coeur d'Alene, Idaho, 83816-0317.
[2] See *Signs in the Heavens*, Chuck Missler, Koinonia House, PO Box D, Coeur d' Alene, Idaho, 83816-0317.

Sir Robert Anderson, in his book *The Coming Prince*, applied this principle of a 360 day calendar year to the 483 years, and made an astounding discovery.[1]

Anderson multiplied the 360 days per calendar year by the 483 years to get 173,880 days. Gabriel was telling Daniel that 173,880 days after the command is given to "restore and rebuild Jerusalem" the Messiah would come. Remember, at the time this prophecy was given, the city of Jerusalem was desolate. Is there a record of a command such as this recorded anywhere in history?

Yes!

In the second chapter of the book of Nehemiah it states:

"In the month of Nisan, in the twentieth year of the reign of Artaxerxes, when wine was before him, I took wine and gave it to the king. Now I had never been sad in his presence before. Therefore, the king said to me 'why is your face sad, since you are not sick?'"

Nehemiah went on to explain that he was sad because he had heard a report that the city of his people, Jerusalem, was still desolate. He requested that he be allowed to go back to Jerusalem and rebuild the city. King Artaxerxes granted his wish on the spot.

The 1990 edition of the Encyclopedia Britannica states that Artaxerxes Longimanus ascended to the throne of the Medo-Persian empire in July 465 B.C.E. By Hebrew tradition, when the day of the month is not specifically stated, it is given to be the first day of that month. So, the day of the decree by Artaxerxes was the first day of the Hebrew month Nisan 445 B.C.E. The first day of Nisan in 445 B.C.E. corresponds to the 14th day of March. This

---

[1] See *The Coming Prince*, Sir Robert Anderson.

was verified by astronomical calculations at the British Royal Observatory and reported by Sir Robert Anderson.

Remember that the prophecy states that 69 weeks of years (173,880 days) after the command goes forth to restore the city of Jerusalem the Messiah will come. If we count 173,880 days forward from fourteenth of March, 445 B.C.E., we come to April sixth, 32 C. E. Again this date was verified by the British Royal Observatory.[1]

Here are the calculations.

March fourteenth, 445 B.C.E. to March fourteenth, 32 C.E. is 476 years.

(1 B.C. to 1 C.E. is one year. There is no year zero.)

476 years x 365 days per year = 173,740 days

Add for leap years = 116 days [2]

March fourteenth to April sixth = 24 days

total = 173,880 days!

What happened on April sixth 32 C.E.? According to Anderson's calculations a humble carpenter rode into the east gate of Jerusalem on a donkey while the crowds cried "Hosanna! Hosanna! Blessed is he who comes in the name of the Lord!"[3] This man's name was Jesus of Nazareth and this was the first day that he allowed his followers to proclaim him as their Messiah. He had previously told them that his day had not yet come.

---

[1]ibid.
[2]Leap years do not occur in century years unless divisible by 400 (therefore, we must add three less leap years in four centuries).
[3] See The New Testament, Luke Chapter 19.

Skeptical? Read on.

Is there any other way to check the accuracy of this date? Yes!

In Chapter three of the gospel written by the Roman physician Luke, it states that in the fifteenth year of the reign of Tiberius Caesar, Jesus was baptized by John the Baptist and began his ministry. The 1990 Encyclopedia Britannica states that the reign of Caesar Tiberius started on August 19, 14 C.E. Most scholars believe Jesus was baptized in the fall season. Consequently, according to Luke, chapter three, the ministry of Jesus started with his baptism in the fall of the fifteenth year of the reign of Caesar Tiberius and (according to most biblical scholars) lasted four Passovers or 3 1/2 years.[1] The first Passover of Jesus' ministry would have been in the spring of 29 C.E. The fourth Passover of his ministry was the day of his crucifixion and would have fallen in the year 32 C.E. The Passover in that year fell on April 10. Remarkably, according to Robert Anderson and the British Royal Observatory, the Sunday before that Passover was April 6!

That day, April 6, 32 C.E., was exactly 173,880 days after Artaxerxes gave the decree to restore and rebuild Jerusalem on March 14, 445 B.C.E! That day was the first day that Jesus of Nazareth allowed his disciples to proclaim him as Messiah!

This prophecy is one of the many proofs that God transcends time and is able to see the beginning of time from the end with incredible precision!

---

[1] The day that a Roman ruler ascends to the throne begins his first year.

Ancient Jews and Daniel's Seventy Weeks

Some of you may be thinking that the application of this prophecy to the Messiah is a Christian contrivance. In fact, most modern rabbis try to deny the messianic application of this prophecy. However, it is well established that ancient Jews believed that this prophecy pinpointed the time of Messiah's coming. In fact, many in the Qumran community (the writers of the Dead Sea Scrolls) believed that they were living in the very generation to which this prophecy pointed![1,2]

In the Babylonian Talmud, compiled between A.D. 200-500, ancient rabbis commented on the time of Messiah's coming and Daniel's seventy weeks prophecy.

Regarding the times referred to in Daniel's prophecy, Rabbi Judah, the main compiler of the Talmud, said:

> "These times were over long ago"
> Babylonian Talmud Sanhedrin 98b and 97a

In the 12th Century A.D., Rabbi Moses Ben Maimon (Maimonides), one of the most respected rabbis in history, and a man who rejected the messianic claims of Jesus of Nazareth, said regarding Daniel's seventy weeks prophecy:

> "Daniel has elucidated to us the knowledge of the end times. However, since they are secret, the wise [rabbis] have barred the calculation of the days of Messiah's coming so that the untutored populace will not be led astray **when they see that   the End Times have**

---

[1] *Biblical Archaeology Review*, Nov/Dec 1992 pg. 58
[2] For a detailed analysis of the ancient Jewish beliefs regarding this prophecy see *The Search for Messiah*, Mark Eastman, M.D., Chuck Smith, The Word for Today, 1993, chapter 6.

already come but there is no sign of the Messiah"[1] (Emphasis added).

Finally, Rabbi Moses Abraham Levi said regarding the time of Messiah's coming:

"I have examined and searched all the Holy Scriptures and have not found the time for the coming of Messiah clearly fixed, except in the words of Gabriel to the prophet Daniel, which are written in the 9th chapter of the prophecy of Daniel."[2]

In the Targum of the Prophets, in Tractate Megillah 3a, which was composed by Rabbi Jonathan ben Uzziel, we read:

"And the (voice from heaven) came forth and exclaimed, who is he that has revealed my secrets to mankind?... He further sought to reveal by a Targum the inner meaning of the Hagiographa (a portion of scripture which includes Daniel), but a voice from heaven went forth and said, Enough! What was the reason?--Because the date of the Messiah was foretold in it!"

In this amazing commentary from the Targum of the Prophets, the writer expressed the knowledge that Daniel's prophecy referred to the coming of the Messiah.[3]

Furthermore, it is well established that the Jews of the Qumran community (the writers of the Dead Sea Scrolls) believed that Daniel's seventy weeks prophecy pinpointed the time of the coming of the Messiah. In fact, many in the Qumran community based their Messianic hope on similar

---

[1] *Igeret Teiman*, Chapter 3 p 24.
[2] The Messiah of the Targums, Talmuds and Rabbinical Writers, 1971
[3] See also the Talmud, tractate Nazir 32b and The Yakult, vol 2, pg. 79d.

chronological calculations. They believed that they were living in the generation to which this prophecy pointed.[1]

Daniel states that the Messiah would be "cut off." The Hebrew word translated as "cut off" is "karath." This word literally means to punish with death by piercings. Jesus was tried and convicted for blasphemy by the Sanhedrin and for insurrection against the Roman empire, both capital crimes, punishable by death. Jesus was then "pierced" by crucifixion on a Roman cross.

The prophecy then states that after the Messiah is "cut off," the people of the prince who is to come would "destroy the city and the sanctuary." In the year 70 C.E., ten legions of Roman soldiers under the Roman general Titus Vespasian destroyed the city of Jerusalem and the Second Temple. Josephus dramatically records that the city was burned to the ground and millions of Jews were killed, cannibalized or starved to death.

A final note on this prophecy. It was written by Daniel at a time when the temple in Jerusalem was desolate. Destroyed in 587 B.C.E., there was no indication in Daniel's day that it would be rebuilt. However, Daniel states that after the temple was rebuilt, the Messiah would come and then "the prince of the people who is to come" would destroy it again. So the Messiah *had to come* to the Second Temple before it was destroyed! In the aftermath of the Roman invasion the people wept in the streets, crying that the temple had been destroyed yet Messiah had not come.

As Jesus rode near to the city of Jerusalem, he stopped and wept, saying:

---

[1]*Biblical Archaeology Review*, Nov/Dec 1992, pg. 58

"If you had known, even you, especially **in this your day**, the things that make for your peace! But now they are **hid from your eyes**! For the days will come upon you when your enemies will build an embankment around you, surround you and close you in on every side, and level you, and your children within you, to the ground; **and they will not leave in you one stone upon another, because you did not know the time of your visitation!**" (Luke 19:42-44)

I believe Jesus held the Jewish people accountable for failing to recognize that the 483 years were up! However, according to the popular view (not the Biblical one) he was not what they expected or wanted in a Messiah. The truth had been hidden from their eyes.

Regarding the Seventy Weeks Prophecy and the Destruction of the Temple

The fact that the Second Temple would be destroyed was undeniably known by the ancient rabbis. And the belief that the Messiah was to come to that temple was also held by most of them. In the Babylonian Talmud (tractate Nazir 32b) we read an interesting discussion about the Second Temple and its destruction. Rabbi Joseph says:

"Had I been there, I should have said to them: is it not written, the temple of the Lord the temple of the Lord the temple of the Lord are these, **which points to the destruction of the First and Second Temples? Granted that they** [the rabbis of the Second Temple period] **knew it would be destroyed, did they know when this would occur?** Rabbi Abaye objected: and did they not know when? **Is it not written, seventy weeks are**

determined upon the people, and upon the holy
city. All the same, did they know on which day?" [1]

This is an obvious reference to Daniel's seventy weeks
prophecy and clearly demonstrates that the rabbis tied this
prophecy to the destruction of the Second Temple. Since,
in the same portion of scripture we read that the Messiah
was to come to that temple, it was entirely reasonable for
the rabbis to believe that the Anointed One (Messiah)
would arrive before its destruction.

"2000 Years with Messiah"

Throughout the ages many rabbis speculated about the
time of the coming of the Messiah. They looked to the
Bible for clues and numerical patterns which they felt were
placed there so that the day of his coming could be known.
As we saw with the seventy weeks prophecy of Daniel,
God was very specific!

The ancient Jewish scholars believed that God worked
in numerical patterns. One of the most intriguing beliefs
was the idea of the "world week." Just as God made the
world in six days and rested on the seventh, so the world
would last 7,000 years. This rabbinical belief came from the
scriptural notion that a thousand years is as a day and a day
is as a thousand years in the sight of God.

"For a thousand years in Your sight are like yesterday
when it is past, and like a watch in the night." (Psalms
90:4)

This same concept was believed by the early Christian
church fathers as well.

---

[1]Babylonian Talmud Section Nazir 32b.

"But, beloved, do not forget this one thing, that with the Lord one day is as a thousand years, and a thousand years as one day." (2 Peter 3:8)

In an early church document called the Epistle of Barnabus, believed by many early church authorities to be authentic, there is a fascinating statement:

"And God made in six days the works of his hands; and he finished them on the seventh day, and he rested on the seventh day and sanctified it. Consider my children what that signifies, **he finished them in six days. The meaning of it is this: that in six thousand years the Lord God will bring all things to an end. For him one day is as a thousand years...therefore children, in six days, that is in six thousand years, shall all things be accomplished...then he shall rest on the seventh day.**"

The ancient rabbis reasoned that since God made the world in six days and rested on the seventh then the world would last 7,000 years. This belief led them to speculate about when the Messiah would come in relation to the 7,000 years.

In the Babylonian Talmud there is a large section (Sanhedrin 96b-99a) in which several prominent rabbis express their opinions on the time of the coming of the Messiah.

Rabbi Elias, who lived 200 years before Jesus wrote:

"The world endures 6000 years: Two thousand before the law, two thousand with the law and **two thousand with the Messiah.**" (Babylonian Talmud, Sanhedrin 96b-99a)

According to this rabbinical commentary the Messiah was to come at the end of the fourth millennium. The Messiah would then be with the people for 2,000 years. After that time, there would come Messiah's 1,000 year reign on earth. If this chronology is true, then our generation is living at the very end of the "2000 years with Messiah!"

The millennium, the 1,000 year reign of the Messiah, is discussed by Rabbi Kattina in the Babylonian Talmud, Sanhedrin 96b-99a:

"The world endures 6000 years and one thousand it shall be laid waste, that is, the enemies of God shall be laid waste, whereof it is said, 'the Lord alone shall be exalted in that day.' **As out of seven years every seventh is a year of remission, so out of the seven thousand years of the world, the seventh millennium shall be the 1000 years of remission, that God alone may be exalted in that day.**"

Later in the Sanhedrin we see another reference to the world week:

"Rabbi Kattina said: Six thousand years shall the world exist, and one thousand it shall be desolate, as it is written, and the Lord shall alone be exalted in that day (a reference to Isaiah 2:2). Rabbi Abaye said: it will be desolate two thousand years, as it is said, after two days will he revive us: in the third day, he will raise us up, and we shall live in his sight (a reference to Hosea 6:1). It has been taught in accordance with Rabbi Kattina: just as the seventh year is one year of release in seven, so is the world: one thousand years out of seven shall be fallow, as it is written and the Lord shall alone be exalted in that day." [1]

---

[1] Sanhedrin 97a & b.

The belief that the Messiah was expected to come after 4,000 years of earth history helps to further explain the great Messianic expectations in the first century. According to Rabbi Abba Hillel Silver, the beginning of the fifth millennium after creation occurred during the early portion of the first century C.E., during the very life and ministry of Jesus of Nazareth!! [1]

Summary

In our examination of Messianic prophecy and ancient rabbinical interpretations, we have seen a number of indicators which pinpointed the time of Messiah's coming. According to the ancient Jewish scholars, the Savior was to come :

1) During the time when membership in the tribe of Judah could confidently be traced (Genesis 49:10)

2) Previous to the demolition of the Second Temple. (Daniel 9:24-27)

3) Before the scepter had departed from Judah, (Genesis 49:10)

4) At the beginning of the fifth millennium after creation. (Babylonian Talmud, Sanhedrin 96-99)

Remarkably, after 70 C.E., none of these criteria would ever exist again!

However, when Jesus was growing up in Nazareth, the scepter had not passed from Judah, the Second Temple was still standing, and the fifth millennium after creation was at

---

[1]*A History of Messianic Speculation in Israel*, Rabbi Abba Hillel Silver, 1927, Macmillan Co., pg. 5-7, ISBN 0-8446-2937-5

hand. Messiah had come, the scepter was removed, then the Second Temple was destroyed, just as Daniel had predicted.

Why Messiah Delayeth His Coming?

After the nation of Israel was crushed by the Roman army, the people were enslaved and dispersed around the world. In their adversity they began to wonder why the Messiah had apparently missed his appointment with the Jewish people.

In the Babylonian Talmud, Sanhedrin 96-99 (written roughly between 200-500 C.E.), the rabbis expressed their disappointment that the Messiah had not come during the expected time. They explain that the delay in the coming of the Messiah was due to the sin of Israel. Otherwise, he would have come around the year four thousand after creation, precisely the time Jesus of Nazareth came.[1]

An astonishing quote is found in Sanhedrin 97b. Rabbi Rabh states:

"All the predestined dates for redemption (the coming of Messiah) have passed and the matter now depends only on the repentance and good deeds."[2]

Here Rabbi Rabh expresses his pain and displeasure that the Messiah did not come when he was expected. From that time onward, according to Rabbi Rabh, the coming of the Messiah depended on the nation of Israel turning to God in repentance.

---

[1] See Edersheim, *The Life and Times of Jesus the Messiah*, Appendix IX., pg. 737-741.
[2] Sanhedrin 97b.

Further along in Sanhedrin we find another astonishing quote:

> "The Tannadebe Eliyyahu teaches: the world is to exist six thousand years. In the first two thousand there was **desolation; two thousand years the Torah flourished; and the next two thousand years is the Messianic era, but through our many iniquities all these years have been lost!**"[1]

Finally, in the Yakult on Psalms 139:16-17 we find the statement:

> "This world is to last 6000 years; 2000 years it was waste **and desolate, 2000 years marks the period under the Law, 2000 years under the Messiah. And because our sins are increased, they are increased.**"[2]

These incredible quotes speak for themselves. The fact that they are recorded in the highly venerated writings of the men who were the heads of ancient rabbinical academies is astonishing. These men, according to their understanding of the Hebrew Bible and the chronology of the day, recognized that the time appointed for the coming of the Messiah had passed.

Was the Bible and its time indicators wrong? Or, had he come?

---

[1]Sanhedrin 97a & b.
[2]Yakult on Psalms 139:16-17, (vol. 2, pg. 129d).

NOTES

CHAPTER 7

WILL MESSIAH COME TWICE?

During the life and ministry of Jesus of Nazareth he declared to his disciples that after his death and resurrection he would come again for his church. This belief, called the "Second Coming," is the great hope of the Christian believer. Virtually all contemporary rabbis, however, reject the idea that the Messiah will come twice, claiming that there is no scriptural or ancient rabbinical foundation for this belief.

During our examination of Messianic prophecy we found that there were "two veins" of prophecy recognized by the ancient rabbis regarding the life, ministry and destiny of the Messiah. Several prophecies predicted a suffering servant who would die for the sins of the people while others predicted a ruling and reigning Messiah.

Virtually no ancient rabbinical writer denied that the subject of the two lines of prophecy was a Messianic figure. However, they simply could not envision how one individual, in one lifetime, could both rule and reign on the throne of David forever and ever, and yet be despised, rejected, suffer and die.[1,2] Consequently, they conceived to split the Messiah in two, creating one Messiah for each line of prophecy. However, as we shall see, one individual could accomplish both lines of prophecy. This requires one

---

[1]Isaiah 9:6.
[2]Isaiah 52:12-53.

119

caveat: He would have to come twice! Is there ancient evidence of a rabbinical belief in just such a solution to this puzzle?

One Messiah or Two?

The "two Messiah" theory is a rabbinical idea which developed in the first or second century C.E. It's not known exactly who first proposed the idea, nevertheless, it is a belief that eventually became firmly rooted in the Talmud. Did this concept develop because of a biblical foundation? Are there biblical prophecies that form the basis for two Messiahs?

During our examination of Messianic prophecy we have found that every one contained a single consistent theme. Whether a "suffering servant" prophecy or one of the "ruling and reigning" scriptures, we find that there is no place where a plural personal pronoun is used in reference to the Messiah. All of the Messianic prophecies use the singular pronoun.

In Deuteronomy 18:15, 18–19 we read:

> "The Lord your God will raise up for you **a prophet** from among your own people, like myself; **him** you shall heed...I will raise up **a prophet** from them from among their own people, like yourself: I will put My words in **his mouth** and **he will speak** to them all that I command **him**; and if anybody fails to heed the words **he speaks** in My name, I myself will call him to account." (J.P.S. 1985)

In this Messianic prophecy, we read that God is going to "raise up a prophet" from among the Jewish people. This is stated twice, in verse 15 and again in verse 18. God then goes on to say that "I will put my words in his mouth and he will speak to them all that I command him." Throughout this Messianic prophecy we do not find the use of pronouns, such as **they** or **theirs,** when referring to this Messianic figure. The only personal pronouns we see used are singular, indicating one Messiah.

In what many believe is the very first Messianic prophecy in the Bible, Genesis 3:15, we read that "**the seed**" of the woman will bruise the head of Satan. Again, this seed is proclaimed with a singular personal pronoun.

In another undisputed prophecy of the Messiah, Micah 5:2, we read:

> "And you, O Bethlehem of Ephrathah, least among the clans of Judah, from you **One shall come forth** to rule Israel for Me. One whose origin is from old, from ancient times." [1]

Again, in this undisputed prophecy of the birthplace of the Messiah, God says through the prophet Micah that "One shall come forth." Neither here nor anywhere else in the Bible is it indicated that two shall come forth. As one examines all the known Old Testament Messianic prophecies we would find that there is no direct scriptural evidence for multiple Messiahs. In each case only singular personal pronouns are used to describe the origin, ministry and destiny of the Messiah.

One Messiah or Two
in the Dead Sea Scrolls

We saw earlier in our discussion of the Qumran text, 4Q521, a reference to a single Messianic figure. In the

---

[1] Micah 5:2 Jewish Publication Society, 1985.

Biblical Archaeology Review, in an article by Hebrew scholars Michael Wise and James Tabor, we find a fascinating analysis of this text.

"**Our Qumran text, 4Q521, is, astonishingly, quite close to this Christian concept of the Messiah. Our text speaks not only of a single Messianic figure...but it also describes him in extremely exalted terms, quite like the Christian view of Jesus as a cosmic agent.** That there was, in fact, an expectation of **a single Messianic figure** at Qumran is really not so surprising. **A reexamination of the Qumran literature on this subject leads one to question the two Messiah theory.** As a matter of fact, only once in any Dead Sea Scroll text is the idea of two Messiahs stated unambiguously." [1]

Wise and Tabor go on to state:

"**In short, there is not much evidence in the previously published scrolls that straightforwardly supports a putative doctrine of two Messiahs... So the text that is the subject of this article (4Q521) is, in speaking of a single Messiah, more the rule than the exception... The Messiah of our text is thus much closer to the Christian Messiah, in this regard, than in any previously published text** and requires us to reexamine the previously, rather restricted, views of Messianic expectations at Qumran."

These recent discoveries from the Dead Sea Scrolls have dramatically changed the belief that the Qumran community was expecting two Messiahs. For the past forty-five years, scholars have felt that the Essenes of Qumran, which was a devout sect of Judaism, were expecting and believed in two Messiahs. However, these new discoveries reveal strong

---

[1]*Biblical Archaeology Review*, November/December 1992, page 60-61.

evidence that the Qumran community was expecting only one Messiah.

The article goes on to state that there is abundant evidence from the Dead Sea Scrolls that the Messiah would in fact be both a ruling, reigning, and triumphant and yet a suffering rejected figure as well. On page 58 the authors state:

> **"There is no doubt that the Qumran community had faith in the ultimate victory of such a Messiah over all evil.** However, a closer reading of these texts reveals an additional theme, equally dominant–that of an initial, though temporary, triumph of the wicked over righteousness. That is, there was the belief among the Qumran community that the Messiah would suffer initial defeat, but that he would ultimately triumph in the end of days."

According to Wise and Tabor, the Qumran community believed that the Messiah would come once and "suffer initial defeat" but at a later time he would "ultimately triumph in the end of days." Although not stated explicitly, this sounds like two appearances of a single Messiah! One appearance in humility and one in glory!

Wise and Tabor go on to show that because of Daniel's seventy weeks prophecy, the Qumran community believed that the Messiah was going to come in the era in which they lived (first century B.C.E.- first century C.E.)

> "We know the Qumran group was intensely interested in this seventy weeks prophecy of Daniel. They tried to place themselves within this chronological scheme as they calculated the eschaton.[1] They must have

---

[1] End of the world which they associated with the coming of the Messiah.

made something out of this Messiah figure who was cut off."

Wise and Tabor admit that the person spoken of in Daniel's seventy weeks prophecy was believed by the Essenes of Qumran to be a Messiah of Davidic descent called the teacher of righteousness. The article goes on to state that :

> "The teacher of righteousness, frequently referred to in the Qumran documents, appears to be a Messiah figure of Davidic descent, who is connected by the writers at Qumran specifically with the figure written about in Daniel 9:25."

When we synthesize the statements by Wise and Tabor regarding the beliefs of the Qumran community, an astonishing, but familiar view of the Messiah comes forth.

This fragment and its interpretation point out that at least some in the Qumran community were expecting a single Messiah, one from the line of David, one whom they called *"the teacher of righteousness."* This belief in a single Messiah was *"more the rule than the exception."* According to Wise and Tabor, the *"Qumran community had faith in the ultimate victory of such a Messiah over all evil."* However, they go on to state that *"a closer reading of these texts reveals an additional theme, equally dominant— that of an initial, though temporary, triumph of the wicked over righteousness. That is, there was the belief among the Qumran community that the Messiah would suffer initial defeat, but that he would ultimately triumph in the end of days."* Finally, Wise and Tabor admit that the Qumran community believed that the Messiah would be "cut off" or killed as prophesied by Daniel's seventy weeks prophecy.

Even more astonishing than the fact that the Qumran community applied both veins of prophecy to a single Messiah, is the fact that they placed the suffering servant prophecies first, followed by the ruling and reigning prophecies. That is, the Qumran community apparently believed (based on biblical chronology) that the Messiah would come during their time, and that he would suffer initial defeat and be cut off (killed), only to return at a later time in glory!

No wonder Wise and Tabor were compelled to state that the beliefs of the Qumran community point to a Messiah that *"is thus much closer to the Christian Messiah."*

So we have discovered sound scholarship that demonstrates that the single Messiah belief was the rule rather than the exception during the first century B.C.E. This new evidence should not be surprising, since it is in perfect agreement with what the Bible has taught for 3500 years. There was to be ONE Messiah!

A Messiah Who Will Both Suffer and Rule Forever?

If there is to be but one Messiah, then we should be able to find additional evidence in the Scriptures that he would fulfill both "veins" of prophecy. The discovery of a passage of Scripture which unites both "veins" of prophecy in the life and ministry of a single individual would be powerful evidence that in fact there is only one Messiah.

As we look through the Tanakh we do find areas where the two "veins" of prophecy are united in the same portion of scripture.

In Isaiah 52:13–53:12, an undeniably Messianic passage, we see the two lines of prophecy united in a description of the same individual. In the Jewish Publication Society version of Isaiah 52:13, we read:

"Indeed, My servant shall prosper, be exalted and raise to great heights."

And yet, in the following verses, we read that this same servant is to be:

"...despised and rejected by men a man of suffering, familiar with disease...But he was wounded because of our sins, crushed because of our iniquities...For he was cut off from the land of the living through the sin of My people, who deserved the punishment...though he had done no injustice and spoken no falsehood...assuredly, I will give him the many as his portion, and he shall receive the multitude as his spoil. For he exposed himself to death and was numbered among the sinners, where as he bore the guilt of the many and made intercession for the sinners."

In this incredible portion of scripture we see a despised, rejected servant, who dies for the sins of the people. Yet, he would also prosper and be exalted and raised to great heights. Both veins of prophecy are here united in the same individual.

In the book of Zechariah we find another Messianic prophecy in which the two veins are again united in the same individual.

"Rejoice greatly, fair Zion; raise a shout, fair Jerusalem. Lo, your king is coming to you. He is victorious, triumphant, yet humble riding on a ass, on a donkey foaled by a she-ass. He shall banish chariots from Ephraim and horses from Jerusalem; the warrior's bow shall be banished. He shall call on the nations to surrender and his rule shall extend from sea to sea and from ocean to land's end." (Zechariah 9:9–10, JPS. 1985)

Here the Messiah is portrayed as a victorious, triumphant king, one to whom the nations will surrender. His rule shall extend from sea to sea, and yet, his arrival will be lowly, riding on a donkey.

Finally, in Daniel 9:24-27, we are told of the specific activities of the coming Messiah. In the Septuagint version[1] we read that he would come to the rebuilt temple, and through his life there would be "an end of sin," "transgressions would be sealed up," he would "blot out iniquities," "bring in everlasting righteousness," "seal up vision and prophecy." However, we discover that he would be "cut off" ("karath" in Hebrew) which is to be killed, thrust through or pierced. The Septuagint translates this word as "shall be destroyed." The person being "destroyed" is specifically referred to as "the Christ," which as we have seen is the Greek translation for the Hebrew word Mashiyach, the Messiah.

Here again, we see the Messianic figure described in exalted terms, accomplishing great things, and yet being killed as well, therefore fulfilling both veins of prophecy in the same portion of scripture!

One Appearance or Two?

Since there is no scriptural evidence for the two Messiah theory, and since it can be shown that both "veins" of prophecy can be united in a single figure, we must now explain how the two veins of prophecy can be fulfilled in the life of one individual.

---

[1]Translated from Hebrew to Greek in 285-247 B.C.E.

How can someone both rule and reign on David's throne "henceforth and forevermore," as Isaiah 9:6 states, and yet, be despised and rejected and die ultimately for the sins of the people? This question is surely a problem that the ancient rabbis struggled over for centuries.

Could the Messiah, in a single appearance, both rule and reign on the throne of David forever and ever, and yet be despised and rejected? Or must he come twice? To answer this question, we must look at both of these lines of Messianic prophecy and logically determine which one must occur first.

When we examine the prophecies of the ruling and reigning Messiah we discover that his reign will last forever and ever. Consequently, we see that this particular line of prophecy has no ending; however, it does have a beginning. Therefore, if this line of prophecy is to be fulfilled in the life of a single individual, one who will also suffer, be rejected and die, then this everlasting triumph must logically be fulfilled last. The ruling and reigning prophecies *could not* be fulfilled first, only to be interrupted by the rejection, suffering and death of the individual, because this would nullify the prophetic theme that the ruling and reigning would be forever and ever and ever.

Since the ruling and reigning prophecies are to continue without interruption, it therefore follows that if there is one Messiah, the suffering servant line of prophecy must be fulfilled first. It cannot logically occur the other way around. This was unforeseen by most of the ancient rabbis, so they interpretively split the Messiah in two, one Messiah for each vein of prophecy.

And since, the Messiah's ruling and reigning mission must come after his rejection, suffering and death, is it logical that both of these veins of prophecy could be fulfilled in a single appearing of a single individual? The answer is obviously no. The Messiah could not come to the earth, be despised, be rejected, suffer and die, and yet rule and reign forever and ever in a single appearance. However, he could accomplish this by appearing twice! In fact, if there is only one Messiah (as the evidence from scripture and the Dead Sea Scrolls shows us) he must accomplish these two destinies in two appearances!

Is there any scriptural evidence that the Messiah would come twice?

The Prophet Hosea and the Two Appearances of Messiah

In the book of Hosea, we see a fascinating prophecy regarding the Messiah and the eventual restoration of the nation of Israel. We read:

> "I will return again to my place till they acknowledge their offense. Then they will seek my face; in their affliction they will diligently seek me. Come and let us return to the Lord; for he has torn but he will heal us; he has stricken but he will bind us up. After two days he will revive us; on the third day he will raise us up, that we may live in his sight."[1]

In this remarkable prophecy, we see a rather peculiar statement by God. He states, *"I will return again to my place till they acknowledge their offense."* What could this possibly mean? Where is God returning from?

In the Bible we are taught that God is a spirit being whose dwelling place is in heaven. Yet, we are also taught that God is omnipresent, existing at all places at once. Prior

---

[1] Hosea 5:15-6:2.

to this passage, God had delivered a sharp rebuke to the Israelites for their unfaithfulness. God then proceeds to declare that because of their unfaithfulness, *"I will return to my place till they acknowledge their offense."*

The context of this scripture seems to indicate that God himself visited planet Earth at a finite point in time and then returned to his place. The passage then implies that God would return to the people after they acknowledge their offense.

This, however, presents an interesting problem. In order for God to return to his place (heaven) he would have to first leave it. It is clear that God, in his omnipresent state, couldn't really leave heaven. However, if he manifested himself in a physical body (in the person of the Messiah) he could leave and "return to [his] place," only to return again a second time to the people.

After returning to what we presume to be heaven, the passage indicates that God would return to the people of Israel when they acknowledge their offense. The word "offense" is *singular*. What singular offense might compel God to withdraw himself from the people of Israel and make such a requirement?

The rejection of the Messiah might be enough to warrant such a response.

As we have seen in this discussion there is no evidence in the scriptures for two separate Messiahs. In fact, new evidence points out that the Qumran community believed in a single Messiah. We have seen that the Messianic prophecies use singular personal pronouns and not plural. We have seen that there is evidence that both lines of prophecy can be united into the life and destiny of a single individual who comes not once, but twice to planet Earth.

This is exactly what the New Testament records regarding the life, mission, ministry and destiny of Jesus of Nazareth.

Did some ancient rabbis believe that the Messiah would come twice?

Yes! Some definitely did.

The Book of Ruth: The Shadows of Two Messianic Appearances

The book of Ruth is perhaps one of the most overlooked books in the Tanakh, yet it is one of the most fascinating prophetic books in the entire Bible. On the surface it is a love story about a Moabite named Ruth, and her marriage to a man from Bethlehem named Boaz. However, rabbinical and Christian scholars find many Messianic "types" or shadows just below the surface of the text.[1,2] For our purpose we will examine an ancient Jewish view of the book that ties it to the Messiah and his coming.

In the Midrash on the book of Ruth there are several fascinating quotes by the rabbis that demonstrate the belief that Messiah would appear on the scene twice.

In the second chapter of the text we read the story of Ruth and her introduction to Boaz. She had been gleaning grain in a field when Boaz meets her and tells her that he has heard of her faithfulness to her mother-in-law, Naomi,

---

[1]See *The Book of Ruth*, Chuck Missler, Koinonia House, PO box D, Coeur d'Alene, Idaho, 83816-0317.
[2]*Types in the Old Testament*, Ada Habershon.

one of his near relatives. During their first meal together we read:

"And at mealtime Boaz said to her, 'Come this way, eat from the bread and dip your morsel in the sour wine.' "

One of the commentators in the Midrash Ruth Rabbah states that:

"'Come this way,' refers to King Messiah, 'eat from the bread,' means the bread of royalty, and 'dip your morsel in the sour wine,' refers to the sufferings of the Messiah, as it is written, 'But he was wounded for our transgressions, bruised for our iniquities' " (a reference to Isaiah 53:5).

After accepting Boaz' invitation, Ruth:

"Sat beside the reapers; and he [Boaz] served her roasted grain; and she ate until she was satisfied, and she had some left over."

According to the Midrash:

"'she sat beside the reapers,'...**means that for a short while the kingship will be snatched away from the Messiah**, as it is written, 'For I will gather all nations to Jerusalem to wage war' (Zechariah 14:2), while the passage, '**and he served her roasted grain,' means that the kingship will be restored to him,** as it is written, '**He shall strike the earth with the rod of his mouth**' (Isaiah 11:4)."[1]

---

[1] This entire discussion is adapted from *The Messianic Hope*, Arthur Kac, pg. 77-78, Baker Books, 1975 ISBN 0-8010-5362-5

So, according to this portion of the Midrash, **the Messiah will come on the scene only to suffer** (*"dip your morsel in the sour wine"*), **then he will have the kingdom temporarily taken from him and he will withdraw,** (*"for a short while the kingship will be snatched away from the Messiah"*). **Then after an unspecified period of time the Messiah will return in power and glory** (*"the kingship of Messiah will be restored to him"*).

In another startling comment in the Midrash Ruth Rabbah, we find Rabbi Berachya, speaking in the name of Rabbi Levi, declaring:

> "It will be with the last deliverer, (the Messiah), as with the first (Moses); as the first deliverer revealed himself first to the Israelites and then withdrew, **so also will the last deliverer reveal himself to the Israelites and then withdraw for a while.**" [1]

The fact that rabbis of the Midrashim, men who were among the most respected Jewish scholars of their time, believed that the Messiah would come to the people of Israel, have his kingdom temporarily removed, suffer, and then return in glory to regain his kingdom, is nothing less than astonishing!

"Our Righteous Anointed is Departed!"

Earlier we read this fascinating observation from the Rosh Hashanah prayer book regarding the coming of the Messiah, his suffering and his reappearance "as a new creature."

---

[1] Midrash Ruth Rabbah 5:6 was compiled in the ninth century A.D. but based on much older material.

"Our righteous anointed is departed from us: horror has seized us, and we have none to justify us. **He has borne the yoke of our iniquities, and our transgression, and is wounded because of our transgression.** He bears our sins on his shoulders, that we may find pardon for our iniquities. **We shall be healed by his wound, at the time that the eternal will create the Messiah as a new creature.** O bring him up from the circle of the earth. Raise him up from Seir, to assemble us the second time on mount Lebanon, by the hand of Yinon."[1,2]

We examined this prayer in some detail in chapter two, however, there are some aspects to this ancient prayer that are pertinent to this chapter.

According to this prayer, the Messiah would apparently depart after an initial appearance (*"Our righteous anointed is departed from us: horror has seized us, and we have none to justify us"*). The context of this prayer seems to indicate that the Messiah has departed as a result of some kind of suffering (*"He has borne the yoke of our iniquities, and our transgression, and is wounded because of our transgression. He bears our sins on his shoulders, that we may find pardon for our iniquities"*).

Finally, as a result of the wounding and suffering of the Messiah, the people of God would be "healed" and justified in the sight of God. This will happen when he, the Messiah (called Yinon), reappears as "a new creature" (*"We shall be healed by his wound, at the time that the eternal will create the Messiah as a new creature."*)

---

[1]Yinon is one of the ancient rabbinical names for the Messiah.
[2]See *The Messianic Hope*, Arthur Kac, The Chapter of the Suffering Servant.

Messiah *Will* Come Twice

In the Midrashic commentaries on the book of Ruth as well as the astonishing prayer just reviewed, we find the belief that the Messiah would come initially to the people and nation of Israel, and yet would be wounded, suffer and apparently depart as a result of this suffering. Following these events, he would return in glory "as a new creature" to heal the people of God and "assemble [them] the second time on mount Lebanon."

This belief in the two comings of the Messiah, as well as the justification of the people through his suffering, is exactly what Jesus of Nazareth claimed would be accomplished through his life.

Truly, Jesus' qualifications for the title Messiah are compatible with ancient rabbinical beliefs as well as the scriptures we have examined. The problem of the two "veins" of prophecy are solved when we realize that both missions are achievable by two appearances of one individual. His first appearance would be characterized by humility and suffering, his second appearance in glory and majesty.

Jesus of Nazareth is the only person in history who can bridge this gap and solve this puzzle.

The Messiah will come **TWICE!**

NOTES

CHAPTER 8

JESUS THE MIRACLE MAN?

Throughout the Hebrew Bible, the ministry of the Messiah is scattered like the pieces of a puzzle. The picture becomes clearer and clearer as we add each additional scripture, finally arriving at the composite picture of the Messiah. An important part of this composite are the signs and wonders that would follow the Messiah. There are many indications in the Hebrew Bible (as well as recent findings in the Dead Sea Scrolls) that the promised deliverer would be a man of miracles.

In the book of Isaiah, we read of the tremendous miracles that would be wrought through the Messiah:

"The Spirit of the Lord God is upon Me, because the Lord has anointed Me to preach good tidings to the poor; he has sent Me to heal the brokenhearted to proclaim liberty to the captives and the opening of the prison to those who are bound." (Isaiah 61:1)

"In that day the deaf shall hear the words of the book, and the eyes of the blind shall see out of obscurity and out of darkness. The humble also shall increase their joy in the LORD, and the poor among men shall rejoice In the Holy One of Israel." (Isaiah 29:18-19)

"Then the eyes of the blind shall be opened, and the ears of the deaf shall be unstopped. Then the lame shall leap like a deer, and the tongue of the dumb sing.

137

For waters shall burst forth in the wilderness, and
streams in the desert." (Isaiah 35:5-6)

Finally, in the Dead Sea Scrolls a newly translated
fragment from the Qumran cave 4, Fragment 4Q521 states:

"the heavens and the earth will obey his Messiah…He
will heal the sick, resurrect the dead, and to the poor
announce glad tidings."

The belief that the Messiah would perform miracles,
such as healing the sick and raising the dead, is well founded
in scripture and was definitely believed by ancient Jews.
Not only would the Messiah perform physical healing, but
spiritual healing as well.

As we look at the ministry of Jesus of Nazareth
recorded in the New Testament Gospels, we encounter a
tremendous number of miracles.

From the very beginning of his ministry, at the wedding
in Cana of Galilee,[1] we see Jesus commanding the forces of
nature. From the turning of water into wine, to the
resurrecting of the dead (such as Jairus' daughter[2] and his
friend Lazarus[3]) we see that Jesus of Nazareth had power
over the laws of nature and was able to perform miracles at
will.

In fact, Jesus of Nazareth went so far as to claim that
the miracles were a sign of his Messiahship.

One day some of the disciples of John the Baptist (who
was in jail at the time) came to Jesus and his disciples and
asked:

---

[1] John .2.
[2] Luke 8:41.
[3] John 11.

" 'Are you the coming One, or do we look for
another?' Jesus answered and said to them, '**Go and
tell John the things that you hear and see. The
blind receive their sight and the lame walk; the
lepers are cleansed and the deaf hear; the dead
are raised up and the poor have the Gospel
preached to them.**' " (Matthew 11:3-5)

In this incredible dialogue Jesus claims that he is "the
coming One," the Messiah. He declares that one of the signs
authenticating his ministry are the miracles that he has done
(he is loosely paraphrasing Isaiah 61).

Regarding these miracles, Jesus stated:

"But I have a greater witness than John's, for the
works which the Father has given Me to finish; the
very works that I do bear witness of Me, that the
Father has sent Me." (John 5:36)

Often after Jesus would perform a miracle he would
instruct the recipient to tell no one because "his hour had
not come." Unlike most of us, he didn't want to draw
attention to himself. Rather, he simply wished to fulfill the
bona fide expectation that Messiah would be a miracle
worker. But there was more to Jesus' ministry than
demonstrations of signs and wonders. Jesus' ministry was
also one of spiritual healing. He truly came "to heal the
brokenhearted."

Speaking to the crowds that followed him, Jesus stated:

"Come to Me, all you who labor and are heavy laden,
and I will give you rest. Take My yoke upon you and
learn from Me, for I am gentle and lowly in heart, and
you will find rest for your souls. For My yoke is easy
and My burden is light." (Matthew 11:28-30)

Skeptics, Miracles, Myths and Scientific Proof

After reading of the miracles of Jesus the skeptic immediately protests that these miracles are myths or events explainable by natural phenomenon. Others will ask, "Can you prove scientifically that these things really happened?"

Many people have difficulty with the idea of miracles. This difficulty arises from the preconceived bias that under normal conditions miracles are impossible. In the natural realm, this is quite true! By definition, a miracle is an event that is unexplainable by "natural law."

Each of the miracles that Jesus of Nazareth performed was in complete defiance of the laws of physics, chemistry and biology. However, all science can tell us is that under *natural* circumstances the miracles recorded in the New Testament are not possible.

Admittedly, miracles cannot happen as a result of explainable phenomenon. However, if the Creator of the universe came to earth as God in human flesh, and if that "God-Man" was the designer of those very laws, then it would be no difficulty at all for him to overrule the guiding principles he set in place.

The charge that the miracles of Jesus were mythical events or stories which were gradually developed over a long time period has no foundation at all when we examine the historical evidence for Jesus and the establishing of the Christian Church.[1]

Most scholars of ancient literature agree that myths are developed over many generations and usually don't

---

[1]See Appendix II

resemble the original events at all.[1] When we examine the historical evidence for the New Testament documents, we discover that they were almost all completed within a generation of the events themselves.[2,3] Consequently, there were many eyewitnesses to the events in Jerusalem who were still living when the Gospels were written. Furthermore, the events were recorded for the most part by eyewitnesses who were willing to die horrible deaths for the conviction that those events were true.

If there was evidence to refute the miracles of Jesus, early enemies of Christianity could have readily destroyed the authority of the New Testament documents. However, there are no such documents from the first century (or any other century for that matter) that refute the recorded accounts of the life or miracles of Jesus. In fact, in the Babylonian Talmud, the writer records that Yeshua, [the Hebrew name for Jesus], was "hanged on a tree for sorcery!"[4] What is interesting about this historical reference to Jesus is that the writer (a non Christian rabbi) makes no attempt to deny that some sort of supernatural events were performed by Jesus. The supernatural events that were associated with Jesus are simply attributed to a demonic source, but not denied. Such a reference, coming from a source unsympathetic to Christianity, is powerful evidence that Jesus did, in fact, perform supernatural feats.

As a former skeptic, trained in the hard sciences and medicine for eleven years, I used to rely heavily on the

---

[1] For a detailed discussion on the development of myths, see *Evidence That Demands a Verdict,* Mc Dowell, Josh. vol., II Here's Life Publishers, San Bernardino,CA.
[2] See *The New Testament Documents, Can You Trust Them?,* F.F. Bruce.
[3] There are fragments of the New Testament that scholars have dated as being as early as the mid first century. Secondly, the entire New Testament, save a few verses, can be reconstructed from the writings of the second century church fathers.
[4] See Appendix II, Historical Evidence for Jesus of Nazareth.

"Can you prove it to me scientifically?" cop–out. The fact is, you can't even use the scientific method to prove that you ate cornflakes for breakfast!

Webster's 1991 Third New International Dictionary defines the scientific method as "the collection of data through observation...and the formulation of an hypothesis (based on those experiments) and the confirmation of the hypothesis formulated."

Using this method you cannot prove that any historical event occurred. This is because historical events are not repeatable. The scientific method cannot be used to prove or disprove any historical event because we cannot measure or collect data after the event has happened.

To prove or disprove an historical event one uses the "legal-historical method" which is the basis of our entire justice system. This approach relies on historical records or accounts in an attempt to reconstruct what transpired in the past. Using this method, I could easily prove that I ate cornflakes this morning, because I could call in witnesses to attest to my claim. The more numerous the corroborating witnesses, the more reliable the evidence and the more likely the historical event took place.

In the case of the miracles of Jesus, there were tens of thousands of witnesses. Consequently, there were tens of thousands of first century Jews who were willing to die the most horrible deaths ever imagined for the testimony they bore. What was that testimony? Simply that Jesus of Nazareth was the Messiah of Israel, God in human flesh, a man who performed hundreds of miracles and, after suffering death on a Roman cross, physically rose from the dead and ascended into heaven.

One of those martyrs, Paul the Apostle, formerly Saul of Tarsus and a student of the great first century sage Gamaliel, described himself as a committed member of the Pharisees, a group that vigorously opposed Jesus. After persecuting the church vigorously for a number of years, he was miraculously converted to a belief in the Messiahship of Jesus of Nazareth. He lived the next three decades serving Jesus and proclaiming that Jesus was the Messiah and that eternal salvation could come only through a belief in him. Like millions of others, Paul was ultimately martyred for his faith in Jesus.

In his defense of the Christian faith, Paul states that there were more than 500 eyewitnesses who saw the resurrected Jesus at one time.[1]

By strict definition, we cannot prove the miracles of Jesus scientifically, but they are highly defensible from a legal-historical perspective.

There are a number of non-believing lawyers who have attempted to refute both the miracles and the existence of Jesus. However, when confronted with the evidence, many became convinced of the historicity of Jesus and the miracles he performed.[2]

Truly the ministry of Jesus, a ministry of physical and spiritual healing, fulfilled the requirements for Messiah set forth by the prophet Isaiah.

---

[1] 1 Corinthians 15:6.

[2] Greenleaf, Simon. *An Examination of the Testimony of the Four Evangelists by the Rules of Evidence Administered in the Courts of Justice.* Grand Rapids; Baker Book House, reprint edition, 1965. Originally published by J. Cockroft & Co., 1874. ,New York.

NOTES

CHAPTER 9

MESSIAH–GOD THE SON?

"I am Alpha and Omega, the beginning and the end, says the Lord, who is, and who was, and who is to come, **the Almighty.**" Jesus of Nazareth (Revelation 1:8)

> "Therefore I said to you that you will die in your sins; for if you do not believe that **I am,** you will die in your sins." Jesus of Nazareth (John 8:24)

Jesus Christ set himself apart from virtually every religious leader in history by making claims such as these. He left us no room for fence sitting. When he declared that he is no less than God, the great "I Am."

In making this claim, Jesus set off a firestorm of debate that began when he claimed equality with God and the storm continues even to this day. He and his disciples clearly maintained that Messiah would be no less a person than God in human flesh. It was these claims that led the ancient rabbis to try Jesus for blasphemy, i.e. claiming equality with God.

The belief that God is a plural being, eternally existent in the three persons of God the Father, God the Son (Jesus) and God the Holy Spirit is called the doctrine of the Trinity. This is one of the foundational beliefs of Christianity and a point of view that is strictly denied by modern rabbis.

This issue is perhaps the most contentious between modern Jewish and Christian scholars. According to virtually all modern Jewish scholars, the belief that the Messiah would be a physical manifestation of God himself, God in human flesh, is a Christian fabrication.[1] Some also claim that there is no Biblical evidence for the plurality of God or the deity of the Messiah. However, a careful examination of the Hebrew scriptures reveals verses where Messiah is called God, verses where Messiah is worshipped and strong evidence that God is a plural being, existing eternally in more than one personage. Finally, there are verses that portray the Messiah as a literal and physical manifestation of God.

Places Where Messiah is Called God

"God With Us"

"Therefore, the Lord himself will give you a sign: Behold, the almah shall conceive and bear a son and shall call his name Immanuel." (Isaiah 7:14, JPS, 1917)

The book of Isaiah is considered by many Jewish scholars to be the greatest book of Messianic prophecy in the entire Bible. In Isaiah, we are told more about the origin, nature, ministry and destiny of the Messiah, than in any other prophetic book. Therefore, it should come as no surprise, that if the deity of the Messiah is to be found in the Bible, it should be found in Isaiah.

In Isaiah 7:14 we are told that a child would be born into the world as a sign to mankind. We saw earlier that the

---

[1] *You Take Jesus, I'll Take God,* Samuel Levine, pg. 12. Hamoroh Press, 1980.

ancient Septuagint translators believed that this child would be born of a literal virgin, the "almah."

The name of the child is to be called Immanuel. The word Immanuel comes from the Hebrew roots "Im", (עַם) which is translated "with" and from the root "El" (אֵל) which is one of the names of God.

The identity of the child "Immanuel" is a point of great contention. However, we examined evidence in chapter three that the child called Immanuel was tied to the same individual called *"the Root of Jesse's stock"*, in Isaiah 11:1 and the *"Mighty God, everlasting Father, Prince of Peace"*, in Isaiah 9:6 verses which were clearly believed to be Messianic.

Although some have found this verse perplexing, it is clearly powerful evidence for the deity of the Messiah. To find a passage that declares that a virgin will have a child whose name will be called "God With Us," must have been startling to the ancients. Yet, it is totally compatible with several other scriptures that indicate the Messiah would be God in the flesh.

"Mighty God"

"For unto us a child is born, unto us a Son is given; And the government will be upon his shoulder; And his name will be called Wonderful, Counselor, Mighty God, Everlasting Father, Prince of Peace." (Isaiah 9:6, N.K.J.)

"For unto us a child is born, a son is given unto us; And the government is upon his shoulder; And his name is called Pele-joez-El gibbor-abi-ad-sar-shalom." (Isaiah 9:5, JPS, 1917)

Isaiah the prophet lived during a time of great despair for the nation of Israel. Yet, in his prophecies there are rays of great hope for the future inhabitants of Israel. In this fascinating verse we see the great Messianic hope declared. Deliverance would come through a "son" who is born physically into the world, a redeemer who would be called "Mighty God."

As we saw in chapter three, this verse was applied to the Messiah by ancient rabbis as well as some contemporary Jewish scholars. Presently most rabbis deny the Messianic application of this verse, and in fact, try to apply it to King Hezekiah of Judah. As we see above, the Jewish Publication Society decided not to translate the names of this Messianic figure into English. Instead the titles are placed in the footnotes and translated as "Wonderful in counsel is God the Mighty, the Everlasting Father, the ruler of Peace."

The key point of contention between Christian and rabbinical scholars is the identity of the one called "Mighty God." When we examine the name in question, "El Gibbor," we find that it is a compound term. The word אֵל "El" is found thirteen additional times in the book of Isaiah. Twelve times the word אֵל is translated by the Jewish Publication Society as "God" and once as "Lord." Furthermore, in Isaiah 46:9 the word "El," אֵל is used as an absolute reference to Jehovah God.

> "Remember the former things of old: That I am God (אֵל) and there is none else; I am God, and there is none like Me." (Isaiah 46:9, JPS, 1917)

In this passage God, אֵל, tells of his ability to declare the beginning from the end, that is, of his existence outside of time and space. Clearly, the prophet Isaiah attached the highest possible meaning to the word אֵל, a meaning no one could seriously apply to a mere mortal, such as King Hezekiah.

Finally, the exact title "El Gibbor" is found in Isaiah 10:21 and is unashamedly translated as "the Mighty God" in the 1985 edition of the JPS Bible.

"A remnant shall return, even the remnant of Jacob, unto the Mighty God (El Gibbor)."

The identity of the person in this passage was not doubted by the ancient rabbis. We saw in chapter three that ancient and even some modern Hebrew scholars believe that the person spoken of is the Messiah.

In another fascinating commentary, the Targum of Isaiah, we find the following statement regarding this passage:

"His name has been called from old, Wonderful Counselor, Mighty God, he who lives forever, the Anointed One (Messiah), in whose days peace shall increase upon us."

Clearly, the redactor of the ancient Targum of Isaiah associated the Messiah with the one to be called Mighty God, Everlasting Father.

The clear Messianic application of Isaiah 9:6 (9:5 Hebrew Bible). coupled with the fact that the title "El Gibbor" is a definite and common reference to the eternal God of Israel, is powerful evidence that, in some supernatural way, the Messiah would be a physical manifestation of God!

"The Lord Our Righteousness"

"Behold the days are coming, saith the Lord, that I will raise unto David a righteous shoot, and he shall reign as king and prosper, and shall execute justice and righteousness in the land. In his days Judah shall be saved, and Israel shall dwell safely; and this is the name whereby he shall be called, THE LORD OUR RIGHTEOUSNESS. (Jeremiah 23:6, JPS, 1917)

Jeremiah the prophet was a witness to the destruction of Jerusalem and the abduction of the people of Israel by the Babylonians. In the midst of his prophetic book, after many chapters of doom and gloom, Jeremiah includes this beautiful prophecy regarding the future redeemer of Israel and the security of the nation under his reign.

This remarkable prediction states that a future king of Israel, from the line of David (a "righteous shoot," sometimes translated the "Branch") will bring justice, righteousness and salvation to Israel, and will be called The LORD (יהוה) Our Righteousness!

The key word in this passage is יהוה, which was translated as "LORD" by the Jewish Publication Society translators in 1917. This word is called the "Tetragrammaton." It is the name of the one who spoke to Moses from the burning bush, the undisputed name for the eternally existent God of Israel, commonly called "YAHWEH."

Who is this person, this "righteous shoot," the one who will reign as king, the one who will save Judah and will be called "THE LORD (יהוה) OUR RIGHTEOUSNESS?"

How could the God of Abraham, Isaac and Moses also be a descendant of David? Why is this person described as a *physical being*, born of the line of David, one who will reign as king "in his days," and yet his name "The Lord (יהוה) Our Righteousness?"

Some might argue that this is simply a prophetic declaration that God will rule over the people of Israel at some point in the future. However, an omnipresent being cannot fit the bill here. Such a being isn't born into time and space with a beginning or end of days. Furthermore, God, in his spiritual, omnipresent state, cannot be a descendant of David. What kind of a being could possibly fulfill such criteria?

The only solution to these requirements would be for God to enter our space-time domain, manifesting himself in a physical body, being born supernaturally as a descendant of David, then to *"reign as king and prosper, and... execute justice and righteousness in the land!"* All these criteria could be solved by God in just such a way. He could be a descendant of David, yet still be the God of Abraham, Isaac and Moses. Furthermore, by entering space–time continuum at a finite point, he would technically have a beginning to his physical earthly days.

Did the ancient rabbis believe that this verse was a reference to the Messiah?

Yes!

This verse is applied to the Messiah in a number of ancient rabbinical writings.[1] Regarding Jeremiah 23:6, the ancient Targum of the Prophets states:

"And I will raise up for David the Messiah the Just."

---

[1] See Babylonian Talmud Babha Bathra 75b, Midrash on Psalm 21.

Rabbi Kimchi (1160-1235 C.E.), a highly respected
rabbi in his time, wrote of this prophecy:

"By the righteous branch is meant Messiah."[1]

Finally, in the Midrash on Psalm 23, it is interesting to
note the Messiah is given a divine designation. He is called,
"Jehovah is a man of war" and "Jehovah our
righteousness."[2] Also in the Midrash on Lamentations 1:16,
the name Jehovah is expressly attributed to the Messiah.

If the ancient rabbis are correct, then the obvious and
startling conclusion is that the Messiah (the righteous
shoot) will be born into the world as a literal and physical
manifestation of God, the great I Am!

For those who might argue that this is not the Messiah,
then the obvious question is again, "to whom else could it
refer?" What other man could deserve the title "THE LORD
OUR RIGHTEOUSNESS?"

A common theme in the verses we have just examined is
that God himself is manifest as a being in time and space.
Some of you may be thinking that this is stretching the
interpretation of these two verses. For those of you who
might argue that it is ridiculous to propose that God would
manifest himself in a physical body, I would like to point
out a number of other places in the Tanakh where God does
just that!

In the book of Zechariah we read of the glorious day of
the LORD when God will make war with the enemies of
Israel and rule among the people in righteousness and truth.

---

[1] Baron, David, *Rays of Messianic* Glory: *Christ in the Old Testament*,
Grand Rapids, MI: Zondervan, 1886
[2] See Edersheim, Alfred, The Life and Times of Jesus the Messiah, Appendix
ix, Mac Donald Publishing Co.

"Then the LORD (יהוה) will come forth and make
war with those nations, as He is wont to make war in a
day of battle. On that day, He will set His feet on the
Mount of Olives, near Jerusalem on the east; and the
Mount of Olives shall split across from east to west,
and one part of the mount shall shift to the north and
the other to the south, a huge gorge." (Zechariah
14:3-4, JPS, 1985)

In this verse we read that YAHWEH will manifest
himself as a physical being, a being with feet, and he will
step on the mount of Olives!

In Genesis 32:24-30 gives a strange story about Jacob
wrestling with God.

"And Jacob was left alone; and there wrestled a man
with him until the breaking of the day. And when he
saw that he prevailed not against him, he touched the
hollow of his thigh; and the hollow of Jacob's thigh
was out of joint, as he wrestled with him. And he said,
'Let me go, for the day breaketh.' And he said, 'I will
not let thee go, except thou bless me.' And he said
unto him, 'What is thy name?' And he said, 'Jacob.'
And he said, 'Thy name shall be called no more Jacob,
but Israel: for as a prince hast thou power with God
and with men, and hast prevailed.' And Jacob asked
him, and said, 'Tell me, I pray thee, thy name.' And
he said, 'Wherefore is it that thou dost ask after my
name?' And he blessed him there. And Jacob called the
name of the place Peniel: 'for **I have seen God face
to face, and my life is preserved.**'"

In this fascinating portion of scripture we find Jacob
wrestling with a man whom he identifies as God.
Furthermore, Jacob apparently recognizes that a man
cannot see God in his glorified state and live. So what form
did God take? The form of a man!

In the book of Genesis we read of an encounter that Abraham had with God.

"And the LORD (יהוה) appeare d to him by the terebinths of Mamre; he was sitting at the entrance of the tent as the day grew hot. Looking up, he saw three men standing near him. As soon as he saw them, he ran from the entrance of the tent to greet them and, bowing to the ground, he said 'My lords, if it please you, do not go on past your servant.' " (Genesis 18:1-4)

The verse states that God appeared to Abraham. What form did God take during this appearance? We know one thing for sure, he did not appear in his glorified, omnipresent, spiritual state. The Bible tells us that no man could survive seeing God in this state.

After receiving the ten commandments on mount Sinai, Moses asked to see the glory of God.

"And he [Moses] said: 'show me, I pray Thee, Thy glory.' And He said, 'I will make all my goodness pass before thee, and I will proclaim the name of the LORD before thee; and I will be gracious to whom I will be gracious, and will show mercy on whom I will show mercy.' And He said, '**Thou canst not see My face, for man shall not see Me, and live.**' " (Exodus 33:18-20)

Obviously, these verses provide a serious challenge to the skeptic that might argue that God has not or will not manifest himself as a man. [1]

---

[1] See also Genesis 3:8 where it is recorded that God was walking in the Garden of Eden.

Places Where Messiah is Worshipped

"One Like Unto a Son of Man"

"And I saw in the night visions, and behold, there came with the clouds of heaven one like unto a son of man, and he came even to the ancient of days, and he was brought near before him. And there was given him dominion, and glory, and a kingdom, that all the peoples, nations, and languages should serve him; his dominion is an everlasting dominion, which shall not pass away, and his kingdom that which shall not be destroyed." (Daniel 7:13-14, JPS, 1917)

Throughout the Bible the people of God are admonished to serve and worship the God of Israel only and not to serve and worship other gods. This is absolutely foundational to the beliefs of the observant Jew.

"Then it shall be, if thou shalt forget the LORD thy God, and walk after other gods, **and serve them and worship them, I forewarn you this day that ye shall surely perish**." (Deuteronomy 8:19)

In the above passages (Daniel 7:13-14) we read of an individual to whom "all the peoples, nations, and languages" will serve. Who is this individual?

We saw earlier that the person identified in this passage is tied to the humble servant of Zechariah 9:9:

"If Israel behaved worthily, the Messiah would come in the clouds of heaven, if otherwise, humble riding on a donkey." (Babylonian Talmud, Sanhedrin 98a)

The author of this portion of the Talmud apparently had little doubt that the person described as the son of man in Daniel 7:13-14 is the Messiah.

A curious aspect to this prophecy, however, is that we are told that "all the peoples, nations, and languages should serve him." The Aramaic word translated "serve," is the word *pelach,* and literally means to serve or to worship; especially in the sense of offering service or worship to God.[1] The very same word, is used six additional times in the book of Daniel, each time with the idea of serving or worshipping God.

In Daniel 3:16-17 the three young Hebrew boys, Shadrach, Meshach and Abed-Nego are summoned to King Nebuchadnezzar because they would not serve (*pelach*) the false gods of Babylon. When the three Hebrews are threatened with death in the fiery furnace for not serving those gods, we find their remarkable response:

> "Shadrach, Meshach, and Abed-Nego answered and said to the king, 'O Nebuchadnezzar, we have no need to answer you in this matter. If that is the case, our God whom we serve, (*pelach*), is able to deliver us from the burning fiery furnace, and he will deliver us from your hand, O king.' " (Daniel 3:16-17)

Later, after King Nebuchadnezzar had discovered that Shadrach, Meshach and Abed-Nego had been rescued from the fiery furnace, he was astonished and began to praise the God of Israel, the God of Shadrach, Meshach and Abed-Nego:

> "Nebuchadnezzar spoke, saying, 'Blessed be the God of Shadrach, Meshach, and Abed-Nego, who sent his

---

[1] See *Wilson's Old Testament Word Studies,* pg. 382, Kregel Publications, 1987.

Angel and delivered his servants who trusted in him, and they have frustrated the king's word, and yielded their bodies, that they should not **serve**, *(pelach)*, nor worship any god except their own God!' " (Daniel 3:28)

Finally, in the seventh chapter of Daniel we are given a description of a dream and vision that Daniel had in the first year of the reign of Belshazzar. Daniel is shown a succession of four beasts which represent the four gentile kingdoms of the earth. These were to be the kingdoms that would arise prior to the coming kingdom of the Most High God, a kingdom that will be everlasting. After a description of the four kingdoms we are told:

"Then the kingdom and dominion, and the greatness of the kingdoms under the whole heaven, shall be given to the people, the saints of the Most High. His kingdom is an everlasting kingdom, and all dominions shall serve*(pelach)*, and obey him." (Daniel 7:27, JPS, 1917)

Here we find the very same Aramaic word, *pelach,* used in reference to "all dominions" (that is, all peoples) serving the Most High God. This is the very same word and the very same activity that Daniel said, in chapter seven, verse 14, would be reserved for the Messiah.

As we can see by these three additional uses of *pelach,* that it represents, in the full sense, the qualities of worship and service to God.

However, God absolutely forbids that we serve or worship anything other than himself, the true and living God of Israel.

Deuteronomy 8:19 tells us what will happen if we worship other gods, *"you shall surely perish."*

Therefore, during the everlasting kingdom of the most High God, it will be forbidden to serve and worship two masters.

According to Daniel 7:14, the group that will serve the Messiah is composed of "all the peoples, nations, and languages." That is, every person on earth will serve him. However, Daniel 7:27 states that the same all inclusive group will be serving "the Most High" God.

Here we encounter a serious dilemma. **If everyone on earth is serving the Messiah, who is left to serve the "Most High" God?**

Has Daniel contradicted himself? How do we reconcile this dilemma?

The obvious solution is that in some supernatural way, the Messiah will be a physical, spiritual and literal manifestation of the eternal God.

In serving (*pelach*) the Messiah, all humanity will truly be serving the Lord, the God of Israel.

"Let All The Angels of God Worship Him"

In the New Testament we find a fascinating verse in the book of Hebrews:

"God, who at various times and in different ways spoke in time past to the fathers by the prophets has in these last days spoken to us by His Son, whom He has appointed heir of all things, through whom also He made the worlds; who being the brightness of His glory and the express image of His person, and upholding all things by the word of His power, when He had by Himself purged our sins, sat down at the right hand of the Majesty on high, having become so much better than the angels, as He has by inheritance obtained a more excellent name than they. For to which of the angels did He ever say: 'You are My Son, today I have begotten You?'[1] And again: 'I will be to Him a Father, and He shall be to Me a Son?'[2] But when He again brings the firstborn into the world, He says: **'Let all the angels of God worship Him.'** " (Hebrews 1:1-6)

In this portion of the book of Hebrews the writer (widely held to be Paul the Apostle) quotes a number of Old Testament passages and then attributes them to Jesus Christ. After describing Jesus as God's *Son* and "*the brightness of His [God's] glory and the express image of His person,*" the writer then quotes Psalm 2 and 2 Samuel 7:14, Messianic verses which *are* found in modern Jewish Bibles. The writer of Hebrews then goes on to state, "*But when He again brings the firstborn into the world, He says: 'Let all the angels of God worship Him.'* " In saying "*He says,*" the writer specifically attributes the words "***Let all the angels of God worship Him***" to God himself. However, if we search the Massoretic text (the official text used by the Jewish Publication Society for printing Bibles) we would search in vain to find this phrase.

Paul, a Pharisee and Apostle of Jesus Christ, was trained by Gamaliel at the most prestigious rabbinical academy in the nation of Israel. He was a keen student of the Bible and could quote the Tanakh from memory on the spot. Memorization of the Tanakh was a requirement of his training. Even through the Middle Ages, young men as young as twelve were expected to memorize the books of Moses, the Torah. Therefore, the verse in question here was very well known to Paul. But where did Paul get this verse?

---

[1] A reference to Psalm 2.
[2] A reference to 2 Samuel 7:14.

The solution to the problem can be found in the Septuagint and the Dead Sea Scrolls. As previously discussed, the Septuagint was a Hebrew to Greek translation that was commenced in 285 B.C.E. During the period from the first century B.C.E. to the second century C.E. it was the most commonly used translation. In fact, many of the New Testament references to the Old Testament are from the Septuagint.

In the book of Deuteronomy we find the following rendering:

> "For I will sharpen my sword like lightning, and my hand shall take hold of judgment; I will render judgment to my enemies, and will recompense them that hate me. I will make my weapons drunk with blood, and my sword shall devour flesh, it shall glut itself with the blood of wounded, and from the captivity of the heads of their enemies that rule over them. Rejoice, ye heavens, with him, and let the angels of God worship him; rejoice ye Gentiles, with his people, and let all the sons of God strengthen themselves in him; for he will avenge the blood of his sons, and he will render vengeance, and recompense justice to his enemies, and will reward them that hate him; and the LORD shall purge the land of his people."
> (Deuteronomy 32:41-43, Septuagint Version)

In this portion of scripture, Deuteronomy 32:41-42, God tells the children of Israel of his power, his glory and how he will render judgment upon his enemies.

In the very next verse we read of someone who will, *"avenge the blood of his sons, and he will render vengeance, and recompense justice to his enemies."*

What is astonishing about this individual is that God states that his angels will worship him. *"Rejoice, ye heavens, with him, and let the angels of God worship him."* This phrase is also found in the Dead Sea Scroll fragment of Deuteronomy 32.

Who is this individual? Why would God have his angels worship him?

It is obvious that this person could not be a mere mortal. No king, priest or prophet could qualify for worship. Not even an angel may receive worship. The Bible tells us:

> "...for you shall worship no other god, for the LORD, whose name is Jealous, is a jealous God." (Exodus 34:14)

And as we saw earlier:

> "Then it shall be, if you by any means forget the LORD your God, and follow other gods, and serve them and worship them, I testify against you this day that you shall surely perish." (Deuteronomy 8:19)

We can see by these verses that God takes worship seriously. The penalty for worshipping anything other than him is death! Consequently, the person sanctioned for worship by God must be a physical manifestation of God himself. The only person that the Bible hints as being a physical manifestation of God is Messiah.

Evidence for Tri-Unity of God

"Hear, O Israel: The LORD our God, the LORD is one!"
(Deuteronomy 6:4, JPS, 1917)

If you are reading this book from the perspective of an observant Jew, at this point a fair degree of agitation may be setting in. The Bible clearly teaches that there is only one God. However, we have seen that the Messiah is called "God with us," the "Mighty God," "The Lord Our Righteousness" and that he is served and worshipped by all people and even God's angels during the kingdom age. We have also found evidence that the Messiah will be a physical manifestation of God or God in the flesh.

How can this be? Could it be that God is in some way a plural being, existing as one God, yet being manifested in more than one personage? Is there scriptural evidence for such a nature? Interestingly, there are many indications of the plurality of the one true God of Israel.

"In the Beginning Elohim"

In the very first verse of the Bible we find a statement which openly declares the plurality of God.

"In the beginning God (אֱלֹהִים) created the heavens and the earth." (Genesis 1:1)

The Hebrew word used for "God" in Genesis 1:1 is the word Elohim, a derivative of the word "El" (אֵל). As we saw earlier, "El" is a commonly used word for God. In the context of Genesis 1:1, there can certainly be no doubt as to who is doing the creating. In the Hebrew language the "im" ending imputes plurality. Therefore, "Elohim" is the plural form of the word "El." Consequently, according to Genesis 1:1, the creator of the Universe, Elohim (אֱלֹהִים) exists as a plural being. If this were not so then the word "El" (אֵל) or perhaps YAHWEH (יהוה) would have been used. However, the Holy Spirit chose to use the word Elohim, the plural form of the name of God in the very first place where the name of God is proclaimed.

"Let Us Make Man in Our Image"

"And God said, 'Let Us make man in Our image, after Our likeness; and let them have dominion over the fish of the sea, over the fowl of the air, and over the cattle, over all the earth and over every creeping thing that creeps on the earth.' " (Genesis 1:26, JPS, 1917)

According to this fascinating verse, man was created by God, Elohim (אֱלֹהִים), in his own image. However, there is something provocative and unexpected in this verse. Prior to the creation of man we find a conversation between God (Elohim) and an unidentified being ("let Us make man in Our image"). Who is this person with whom God is speaking?

This person or intelligent being has some attributes that we can glean from the text. First, the being is able to speak with God "on his turf" that is, in the realm of timeless eternity. We know this because man had not yet been created. Therefore, God was not talking to an earthly intelligence. He must have been speaking to a being that exists in the supernatural, eternal realm.

Secondly, this being apparently has the same kind of creative ability as God ("Let *Us* make"). This describes a cooperative effort between Elohim and the person with whom he is speaking.

Finally, the likeness or image of this being is comparable to God's ("In Our image, after Our likeness").

When confronted with this passage, modern rabbis often claim that God is speaking to the angels. However, this explanation fails to recognize a number of problems.

First, there is no indication in the Bible that angels can create life. Secondly, nowhere is it indicated that angels are made in the image of God. Finally, there is no indication that mankind was made in the image of angels either![1]

We may conclude that the person with whom Elohim is conversing lives in the eternal realm, has his creative power and exists in the image or likeness of God. No angel, no man, no created being in heaven or on earth could possibly fit this criteria. What is the solution? It may be found in one of the strongest monotheistic passages in the entire Tanakh.

> "Hear, O Israel: The LORD our God, the LORD is one!" (Deuteronomy 6:4)

In this verse we are told that God is One. However, when we examine the Hebrew word "*echad,*" translated here as "one," we discover an interesting meaning. The Hebrew word "*echad*" comes from a Hebrew root "*achad*" which means "to unify" or "to collect together." The word in question means literally a "united one."

We can get a better feel for its usage by examining a couple of additional verses.

> "Therefore shall a man leave his father and his mother, and shall cleave unto his wife, and they shall be one (*echad*) flesh." (Genesis 2:24 , JPS 1917)

Regarding the people of the earth after the flood we read:

---

[1] Some scholars argue that the plurality implied in the name Elohim is a plurality of majesty. However, in this section we find Elohim acting as a plural being in the creation of man.

"And the Lord said: They are one (*echad*) people, and they have all one language." (Genesis 11:6, JPS, 1917)

In each of these verses we see the idea of separate persons viewed as a unified "one." The man and woman become "one flesh." The people of the earth become unified together as "one people." This unification in these verses obviously does not mean that they physically unite into a single being. The individuals still retain their personal identity and distinct personage. The word "one" here implies a "compound unity."

It is in this sense that we can understand the "One God" in Deuteronomy 6:4.

In the Hebrew language the word "yachiyd" (pronounced "yaw-kheed") is used to indicate "one and only one." This word is frequently translated into the English word "only." However, it literally means "only one" or "solitary one." It is a word which implies an indivisible one as opposed to the compound unity implied by the word "ekhawd."

In the following verses we see some of the uses of the word "yachiyd."

"And he said, 'take now thy son, thine only ["Yachiyd"] son, whom thou lovest, even Isaac and get thee into the land of Moriah; and offer him there for a burnt offering upon one of the mountains which I will tell thee of.'"[1] (Genesis 22:2, JPS, 1917)

---

[1]A fascinating aspect to this verse is that the Holy Spirit inspired Moses to use a word that means "one and only one" indicating that God recognizes only one of Abraham's sons, Isaac. God had given Abraham a promise that through his seed all the nations would be blessed (Genesis 13:16.). Abraham at the time that God told him to sacrifice his "only son," had an

"For I was a son unto my father, tender and an only one ["Yachiyd") in the sight of my mother." (Proverbs 4:3, JPS, 1917)

"And I will pour upon the house of David, and upon the inhabitants of Jerusalem, the spirit of grace and of supplications: and they shall look upon me whom they have pierced, and they shall mourn for him, as one mourneth for his only [Yachiyd] son, and shall be in bitterness for him, as one that is in bitterness for his first born." (Zechariah, 12:10)

If God was an indivisible unity, as opposed to a compound unity implied by "ekhawd", then surely the Holy Spirit would have inspired Moses to use the word "Yachiyd."

The infinite, eternal God of Israel is in some sense, a unification of two or more persons or a compound unity!

The "Creators" of the Universe?

The plurality of the Creator seen in Genesis 1:1 has been dismissed by some as simply a description of God's plural majesty. However, the plurality of the Creator is also seen in a number of very provocative verses.

In Ecclesiastes 12:1 we read:

"Remember also thy **Creators** in the days of thy youth, While that the evil days come not, Nor the years have arrived, that thou sayest, 'I have no

---

older son named Ishmael. However, God did not recognize Ishmael as the son of the promise, the one through whom the Messiah would come. God told Abraham that Isaac was to be the son of the promise (the one through whom the Messiah would come, Genesis 17:19).

pleasure in *them*.'" (Young's Literal Translation, 1898)

The word Creators is a plural form of the word "bara," which means to create out of nothing.[1,2]

The notion of plural Creator is also seen in Isaiah 54:5, where the prophet states:

> "For thy Maker is thy husband, Jehovah of Hosts is His name, And thy Redeemer is the Holy One of Israel, 'God of all the earth,' He is called." (Young's Literal Translation, 1898)

In this verse the word "Maker" is the plural form of the word "asa," which means to form or make from existent materials.

Next to God's work of salvation, the creation of the universe is esteemed by the rabbis as His greatest achievement. So it astonishing to find verses which speak of a plural Being, "Elohim," and the concept of "Creators" or "Makers" for the universe.

The Feet of God!

In the book of the prophet Zechariah, written at least four hundred years before the birth of Jesus, we are given a glimpse of the last days:

> "Then shall the LORD go forth, and fight against those nations, as when he fought in the day of battle. And His feet shall stand in that day upon the mount of Olives, which is before Jerusalem on the east, and the mount of Olives shall cleave in the midst thereof

---

[1] The is the same word used in Genesis 1:1 "Elohim created (bara)."
[2] In most English translations this plurality is not carried through. However, it is there in the original Hebrew text.

toward the east and toward the west, and there shall be
a very great valley; and half of the mountain shall
remove toward the north, and half of it toward the
south." (Zechariah 14:3-4)

In this portion of Scripture we are told that Yahweh
("LORD") will manifest himself in time and space in a body
with feet and stand on the mount of Olives.

In the book of the Acts of the Apostles, the identity of
this person is further clarified in chapter one. The scene
depicted is forty days after the resurrection of Jesus. He
has just told His disciples that He is going to send the Holy
Spirit. In the very next verse we read:

"And when he had spoken these things, while they
beheld, he was taken up; and a cloud received him out
of their sight. And while they looked steadfastly
toward heaven as he went up, behold, two men stood
by them in white apparel; Which also said, 'Ye men of
Galilee, why stand ye gazing up into heaven? T his
same Jesus, which is taken up from you into heaven,
shall so come in like manner as ye have seen him go
into heaven.' Then returned they unto Jerusalem from
the **mount called Olivet**, which is from Jerusalem a
Sabbath day's journey." (Acts 1:9-11)

This is one of those places where a casual reading of the
text fails to uncover an astonishing nugget which reveals the
supernatural engineering of the biblical text.

In Acts, chapter one, the scene is the ascension of Jesus
Christ into heaven. Can you imagine the look on the
disciples faces as they watched this event. As they are
staring in awe, two angels (men in white apparel) tell the
disciples that Jesus' return will be, in effect, a re-run of His
ascension into heaven. Then the Holy Spirit inspired Luke,
the author of Acts, to insert a seemingly insignificant

commentary that they returned "unto Jerusalem from *the mount called Olivet.*"

In other words, when Jesus comes a second time, He will descend from heaven and set His feet on the place from where He ascended – the mount of Olives!

The Book of Zechariah states that this event will be accomplished through a physical manifestation of Yahweh. The New Testament says it's Jesus. Either we have an irreconcilable contradiction, or Jesus and Yahweh must be One and the same!

Messiah-God the Son!

In this chapter we have examined a number of perplexing yet provocative passages of scripture. When examined individually, they seem confusing, even contradictory. However, when we synthesize them, a remarkable solution results.

Most modern rabbis claim that there is no evidence that the Messiah would be a physical manifestation of YAHWEH (יהוה). However, we have found verses in which the Messiah is specifically called God.

In Isaiah 7:14, the Messiah is called Immanuel, meaning "God with us." In Isaiah 9:6 he is called "The Mighty God, Everlasting Father, Prince of peace." Finally, in Jeremiah 23:6, the Messiah is called the most Holy name of all, "THE LORD (יהוה) OUR RIGHTEOUSNESS."

Daniel 7:14 tells us that during the everlasting kingdom, the Messiah and the Most High God will both be served and worshipped by everyone on earth. However,

Deuteronomy 8:19 tells us that if we *serve and worship* anything other than God we "shall surely perish."

In Deuteronomy 6:4 we find the plural nature of God again expressed in the word *echad* which implies that God is a compound unity.

Finally, we find God (Elohim) having a conversation with someone regarding the creation of man. God stated, "Let Us make man in Our image, after Our likeness."

How can this all be true, and yet there be only one true God?

The only possible answer is that God is a plural being manifested in at least two persons, one of which must be the Messiah!

In the entire history of the world there is only one person who has even made claims compatible with the criteria we have examined.

His name was Jesus of Nazareth.

During the life of Jesus of Nazareth, he claimed equality with God (יהוה).

In fact, he was tried and condemned by the Sanhedrin for this very claim. Yet, the claims of Jesus were totally compatible with the scriptural paradoxes we have just examined.

Jesus of Nazareth declared in John 10:30:

"I and My Father are one." [1]

The Greek word that Jesus used in this verse is again, a compound "One," indicating a union of two or more persons in one God.

Jesus of Nazareth declared that he was the "I Am," the One who spoke to Moses from the burning bush, "for *if you do not believe that I am, you will die in your sins."* (John 8:24)

One day Jesus astonished the Jewish leadership in the following discourse:

> " 'Your father Abraham rejoiced to see My day, and he saw it and was glad.' Then the Jews said to him, 'You are not yet fifty years old, and have You seen Abraham?' Jesus said to them, 'Most assuredly, I say to you, before Abraham was, I AM.' " (John 8:56-58)

Apparently there wasn't much doubt among the Jewish leadership regarding just exactly what Jesus was claiming. In the very next verse we read:

> "Then they took up stones to throw at him; but Jesus hid himself and went out of the temple, going through the midst of them, and so passed by." (John 8:59)

The disciple Thomas, upon seeing Jesus alive after the resurrection, fell down, worshipped him and declared, "my Lord and my God." [2]

---

[1] When Jesus quoted the verse in Genesis 2:24, "The two shall become one flesh," He used the same Greek word as when He stated, "I and my Father are One," showing that He understood and was reaffirming the compound unity He had with the Father.
[2] John 20:28.

To his disciple, Philip, Jesus declared that he was the very image of God.

> "Jesus said to him, 'Have I been with you so long, and yet you have not known Me, Philip? He who has seen Me has seen the Father; so how can you say, Show us the Father.' " (John 14:9)

In the New Testament, the Immanuel prophecy is specifically applied to Jesus.

> " 'Behold, a virgin shall be with child, and bear a Son, and they shall call his name Immanuel' which is translated, 'God with us.' " (Matthew 1:23)

Jesus accepted service and worship from his disciples, something Deuteronomy 8:19 stated was to be reserved only for God.

Jesus declared that he lived in heaven, in eternity, prior to the creation of the world.

> "And now, O Father, glorify Me together with Yourself, with the glory which I had with You before the world was." (John 17:5)

The New Testament declares that Jesus was the Creator of all things.

> "In the beginning was the Word [Jesus] and the Word was with God, and the Word was God. He was in the beginning with God. All things were made through him, and without him nothing was made that was made.... And the Word became flesh and dwelt among us, and we beheld his glory, the glory as of the only begotten of the Father, full of grace and truth." (John 1:1-3, 14)

According to the apostle John, Jesus "was in the beginning with God." Consequently, Jesus must have been a party in that conversation with God (Genesis 1:26) before the creation of man.

The plural nature of God, the descriptions of the Messiah as God and the fact that the Messiah will be served and worshipped as God, all indicate that the creator, Elohim, was speaking to the Messiah, the One he calls "My Son,"[1] before they created man in their image.

Did the rabbis of ancient times believe that the Messiah would be a physical manifestation of God?

According to Alfred Edersheim:

"The Messiah expected was far above the conditions of the most exalted of God's servants, even his angels; in short, so closely bordering on the Divine, that it was almost impossible to distinguish him therefrom."[2]

Within one generation of the life of Jesus, tens of thousands of Jews and gentiles were willing to die for the belief that Jesus fulfilled these criteria and therefore that he was God in the flesh!

---

[1] Psalm 2.
[2] Edersheim, Alfred, *The Life and Times of Jesus the Messiah*, vol. pg. 179.

NOTES

CHAPTER 10

WHO MOVED THE STONE?[1]

"Now after the Sabbath, as the first day of the week began to dawn, Mary Magdalene and the other Mary came to see the tomb, and behold, there was a great earthquake, for an angel of the Lord descended from heaven and came and rolled back the stone from the door and sat upon it. His countenance was like lightning, and his clothing as white as snow. And the guards shook for fear of him, and became like dead men. But the angel answered and said to the women, 'Do not be afraid, for I know that you seek Jesus who was crucified. He is not here, for he is risen, as he said. Come see the place where the Lord lay. And go quickly and tell his disciples that he is risen from the dead!' " (Matthew 28:1-7a)

"But if there is no resurrection of the dead, then Christ is not risen. And if Christ is not risen, then our preaching is in vain, and our faith is also in vain."
(I Corinthians 15:13-14)

The resurrection of Jesus Christ, recorded in the New Testament gospel accounts and validated here by Paul the Apostle, is either the greatest event in the history of the universe or it is the greatest hoax perpetrated in the history of mankind. The resurrection of Jesus Christ is an issue that has divided Christianity and Judaism since the day it occurred, the seventeenth of Nisan, around the year 32 C.E.

---

[1]The inspiration for this chapter and its title are borrowed from the classic book, *Who Moved the Stone?*, by Frank Morison.

175

From the onset the Sanhedrin began to attack and deny the truthfulness of the event. We are told in the gospels that the Pharisees first told the guards assigned to secure the tomb to report that the disciples had stolen the body. During the last nineteen centuries skeptics and scholars have been trying to explain away the empty tomb. Since the initial "stolen body" theory was put forth, a number of "natural explanations" for the empty tomb have been proposed.

I believe, like Paul, that the truth of Christianity absolutely stands or falls on the resurrection of Jesus Christ.

As he said:

"If there is no resurrection of the dead, then Christ is not risen, and if Christ is not risen, then our preaching is in vain, and your faith is also in vain." (1 Corinthians 15:13-14)

In this chapter we will examine the evidence for the resurrection as well as several of the alternative explanations for the empty tomb. The hope is that this will stimulate the reader to further study in this area.

Can You Prove It Scientifically?

One of the first questions about the resurrection we need to deal with is the question of "scientific proof." Many people, when confronted with the resurrection of Jesus will ask, "Can you prove scientifically that the resurrection happened ?"

Many people believe that if something can't be proven scientifically, then it must not be true. This is the great twentieth-century cop–out. Our modern generation has been so influenced by modern scientific and technological discoveries that we have collectively come to believe that the scientific method is the ultimate crucible of inquiry. As we saw earlier in our discussion of miracles, the scientific method involves the observation of repeatable events and the formulation of a hypothesis based on those observations. History, however, is not something that is repeatable. No one can study history in the laboratory.

The disciples claimed that Jesus rose. The Pharisees claimed that he didn't. The question of the resurrection is more correctly a problem for the courtroom, with the use of the legal historical method, rather than the laboratory. Because of its inherent limitations we cannot even use the scientific method to "prove" that George Washington was the first president of the United States. However, using the legal historical method, one could easily establish this fact. Therefore, it is the legal historical method we will use to evaluate the evidence.

The first link in the chain of events we will examine is the trial of Jesus.

The Trial of Jesus

During the last week of his life, Jesus had been teaching openly in Jerusalem. He had stirred the wrath of the Sanhedrin because he rode into Jerusalem on a donkey as the crowds yelled "Hosanna, Hosanna, blessed is he who comes in the name of the Lord!" In doing this he openly proclaimed himself as the Messiah in the fulfillment of Zechariah 9:9. Jesus had criticized the leaders for being dishonest, prideful, materialistic, selfish and spiritually blind. He accused them of making a profit from the marketing of animals for sacrifice in the Temple. He had become a tremendous threat to their personal finances as well as their political status. Finally, Jesus declared equality with God. Consequently, the Sanhedrin decided that he had to die.

The Sanhedrin had obtained a promise from Judas Iscariot that he would bring them to the place where Jesus and his disciples would stay on the eve of the Passover. Every night that week Jesus and the disciples left Jerusalem and spent the night in Bethany. However, on the night of the Passover, Jesus took his disciples up to the Garden of Gethsemane. Most scholars believe that the arrest of Jesus occurred sometime around midnight that night.

There are many aspects of the trial of Jesus that are, to say the least, provocative. According to Jewish law it was illegal to try a capital case after dark.[1] It was also forbidden to try a case after the testimony of the initial witnesses was found to be conflicting.[2] Yet, when we examine the witnesses who testified against Jesus, we see that even the Sanhedrin recognized that their testimony disagreed.[3]

The charges against Jesus were also very unusual. He was not being brought up on charges for something he did, but for something that he claimed! He claimed to be the Messiah and he claimed to be the Son of God. Usually, when someone makes an unprovable assertion he is simply dismissed as a lunatic. Many people claim to be God, the Messiah, the King or Queen of England or even aliens from outer space. These claims are usually ignored. But Jesus of Nazareth is one of the very rare people in history to be tried, in a capital case, for simply making a claim about himself.

---

[1]Babylonian Talmud, Sanhedrin.
[2]ibid.
[3]Matthew 26:59-61.

As we saw previously, the Jews had lost their ability to carry out capital punishment around the year 6-7 C.E. when Caponius was placed as procurator of Judea.[1]

As a result of their inability to institute capital punishment, they had to go to the Roman procurator to arrange for the death penalty. They clearly wanted Jesus dead. If they simply wanted Jesus just to be locked away they could have done that on their authority. So the Sanhedrin did the only thing they could, they brought Jesus to Pontius Pilate.

It is interesting that after interrogating and flogging Jesus, Pontius Pilate found him innocent. John records Pilate's remarkable declaration:

"Then Jesus came out wearing a crown of thorns and a purple robe, and Pilate said to him, 'Behold the Man.' Therefore when the chief priests and officers saw him they cried out, 'Crucify him! Crucify him!' And Pilate said to them, 'You take him and crucify him, for I find no fault in him.' " (John 19:5-6)

In telling them to crucify Jesus themselves, Pilate was either being sarcastic or he had forgotten that the Jews could not carry out capital punishment. Clearly Pilate did not want to crucify Jesus, so he gave the assembled crowd an alternative. According to custom, Pilate would release one prisoner on the Passover. He was no doubt certain that the crowd would prefer their king to a convicted murderer named Barabbas. But at the urging of the religious leaders, the crowd called for Barabbas to be released and for Jesus to be crucified.

The crucifixion occurred at nine in the morning. The gospels claim that the sky went black from noon until three p.m. This episode of total mid-day darkness is supported by several extra biblical historical sources![1] Jesus died on the cross at approximately three in the afternoon on Passover.

Where were the disciples at that time? After the arrest of Jesus, the gospel records tell us that John and Peter were following "a far off" as Jesus was taken into the residence of the High Priest where his trial occurred. Later, at the foot of the cross, we find a handful of women and John, the lone disciple of Jesus still present to the bitter end.

The disciples clearly believed that Jesus was the Son of God and the Messiah. Yet, when faced with death they fled, probably to the city to Bethany. Certainly, they were a dejected, scared, shattered group of men. They had seen their hope of the Messianic kingdom murdered on a Roman cross, a form of death usually reserved for only the worst criminals. Their Messiah had been despised, rejected, beaten with many stripes and had poured out his soul unto death.

If anyone doubts the fact that Jesus of Nazareth really did die on a cross, we know from extrabiblical sources that his death on the cross is an historical fact. First century historian Josephus and the Babylonian Talmud both affirm and validate the historicity of the crucifixion and death of Jesus of Nazareth.[2] Therefore, those who would argue that Jesus and his death on the cross are myths, do so in the face of unsympathetic, therefore, reliable historical evidence. To find the historical existence and death of Jesus recorded in these sources clearly unsympathetic to Christianity is powerful evidence for the historical facts. When the evidence is weighed, the truth of the death of Jesus by

---

[1]See Appendix II, Historical Evidence for Jesus of Nazareth.
[2]ibid.

crucifixion can be established beyond doubt as an historical fact.

When one reads the account of the arrest, trial, crucifixion, death and burial of Jesus, nothing is present apart from the nuts and bolts of a true story. There is nothing that appears contrived like a myth or fairy tale. The frightened disciples, the reluctance of Pilate, the urgency of the Sanhedrin to get Jesus quickly tried, condemned and crucified early in the morning before most of the supporters of Jesus had come to town for their business, all seems very believable.

The facts speak for themselves. Jesus of Nazareth was tried, crucified on a Roman cross and died.

Early Sunday Morning

The New Testament records that early Sunday morning a small contingent of women who followed Jesus were on their way to the tomb, and that it was very early. These women had spent a tremendous amount of time with Christ. They had ministered to him for three years and had seen the most amazing miracles performed by him. They believed in their hearts and minds that Jesus was not just a prophet, but also the very Son of God. But, they had also seen him murdered three days earlier.

The pain and the sorrow these women were experiencing is unimaginable. Certainly they weren't expecting anything other than a tomb guarded by Roman soldiers. We read in the gospels that the women were discussing among themselves, "Who will we get to roll away the stone for us?" Consequently, an empty tomb was the farthest thing from their minds. When they arrived at the tomb and found the stone rolled away, they looked inside and found no body. What a shock that must have been! They must have thought, "Great! They've killed him, and now they've taken the body."

When we read the gospel accounts of the women at the tomb, we don't find anything in their character or their actions that was unusual. They were probably hysterical when they found the tomb empty. However, at some point they met what they claimed was a risen Jesus of Nazareth. The women then go to the disciples and report that the tomb was empty and Jesus is risen!

What happened to the body?

One thing is certain, the women did not and could not have removed it.

The Stolen Body Theory

From the very first day of the resurrection of Jesus, the "stolen body theory" was put forth by the Sanhedrin as the cause for the empty tomb.

> "Now while they were going, behold, some of the guard came into the city and reported to the chief priests all the things that had happened. When they had assembled with the elders and taken counsel, they gave a large sum of money to the soldiers, saying, 'Tell them, "His disciples came at night and stole him away while we slept." And if this comes to the governor's ears, we will appease him and make you secure.' So they took the money and did as they were instructed; and this saying is commonly reported among the Jews until this day." (Matthew 28:12-15)

For many years I was comfortable with the stolen body theory. Like many skeptics I had comfortably explained away the resurrection as a hoax, executed by a clever band of zealots in the first century. However, when I undertook a more detailed examination of the evidence that comfort level quickly dissipated.

There are several problems with the stolen body theory.

When we read of the lives of the disciples we find them to be simple men, whose faults are demonstrated throughout the text of the New Testament. They are at times portrayed as prideful, fearful and foolish. They display the same simple desires for prestige and personal comfort that any normal person would seek. If they did steal the body, then they did so at tremendous personal cost. There is no evidence from the New Testament or history that these men acquired any worldly personal gain from becoming Christians. In fact, history shows that the first century Christians were willing to give up their worldly possessions, suffer severe hardship and die by the most horrible methods ever invented by men. Why? For the belief that Jesus of Nazareth *did rise* from the dead! Finally, the disciples allowed their faults and failures to be portrayed in parchments that they knew were being copied and spread all over the known world. Would men like this make such sacrifices to prop up a known and personally very dangerous lie? But even to concede the possibility that the disciples stole the body creates more difficulties than it solves.

In order to steal the body the disciples would have to find a tomb in pitch dark, the location of which, by all accounts, the disciples had not yet seen. Next, they would have to get past the Roman guard which was usually a group of sixteen men. The Roman guards typically slept in shifts of four hours. Twelve were awake and four were sleeping at all times.

Next, they would have to move a stone weighing approximately one and a half to two tons, without disturbing or being noticed by four sleeping and twelve fully awake soldiers. It was also a capital crime to break the Roman seal that was certainly placed on the tomb. Who broke this seal? The guards? Not at the risk of death. The disciples? Impossible. This seal was guarded with the utmost care. To propose that all the guards were sleeping is also unreasonable. It was a death penalty offense to sleep when you were on guard as a Roman soldier. In fact, a Roman soldier would lose his life if an object he was guarding was stolen or removed. Consequently, they took their work very seriously. They did not sleep on duty.

Next, the disciples had to carry the corpse and dispose of it, again going unnoticed. Finally, they had to be back into the house in time to act surprised when the women returned from the tomb, make sure that their stories were straight and then they had to live anywhere between six and sixty-eight years with the knowledge that hundreds of thousands of people were dying for the belief in the resurrection, a story that they had made up!

Now it's obvious that this explanation just doesn't fit with what we know about the church. We know that after the arrest of Jesus at least nine of the disciples fled for their lives. We know that Peter, although he didn't flee, had denied Jesus three times. However, after living for about thirty years as a leader in the church, Peter was himself crucified for his faith in Jesus.

We know that fifty days after the resurrection, on the day of Pentecost, those same cowardly disciples were in the middle of Jerusalem proclaiming that Jesus had risen from the dead! They announced this in the most dangerous place to make such a claim, in Jerusalem.

Obviously, these men had been radically changed. The witness of the early church is totally unexplainable if the body had been stolen. If the body had been stolen, one cannot account for the growth of the church or the persecution that they were willing to suffer. Human nature drives us toward the goal of personal survival. How then can we explain the willingness to die such horrible deaths? Something radical, something incredible, something life changing had to happen to these early Christians to cause them to willingly suffer in the manner so well recorded by history.

"Who Would Die For a Lie?"

When confronted with the question of the martyrdom of the disciples, some would argue that perhaps they were willing to die for the lie that they had created. Perhaps after people started dying for this false hope they were afraid of the consequences of coming forth with the truth. Some skeptics argue that many people have willingly died for a lie, so why not the disciples? The kamikaze pilots of World War II willingly flew their planes into the American Pacific fleet for the promise of great glory in the afterlife. Why was this any different?

Again, this argument runs headlong into some insurmountable problems. Certainly many people have died for causes that were in fact lies. The Jonestown massacre and the Branch Davidian compound burning are recent examples. However, the kamikazes, Branch Davidians and the people of Jonestown all had something in common. They all believed that they were dying for a true and noble cause.

The early Christian church, within less than a decade of its inception, suffered some of the most horrible persecution ever recorded by history. Within a generation of the discovery of the empty tomb, tens of thousands of Christians were burned at the stake, crucified, stoned, eaten by wild beasts, beheaded, boiled in oil and even cooked alive in large metal pans.[1] All this for the belief that Jesus of Nazareth had risen from the dead.

However, there was usually an out available for the people facing martyrdom by the Romans. If the person under inquiry would simply renounce faith in Jesus (and therefore their belief in the resurrection) he would be spared the horrible death that awaited. This option was certainly offered to the disciples as well. If just one of them would recant the story of the resurrection, then this fledgling religion would have folded immediately and registered barely a blip on the screen of history.

However, this is not what happened. The church spread rapidly in the face of unimaginable persecution. According to Foxe's Book of Martyrs eleven of the twelve apostles were martyred. For the disciples to give up their worldly possessions and whatever status and security they had attained, and to willingly die for a story they knew was false, defies the natural human drive for personal survival as well as all logic. Additionally, such a death bears no resemblance to the deaths of the kamikazes, Branch Davidians and the people of Jonestown. These groups died for something they thought was true. The disciples would have died for something they knew was a lie! No sane person would do this.

When the spikes were about to be nailed into the hands and feet of a disciple or when the sword was about to be laid to the neck, they could have simply recanted the story,

---

[1]See Foxe's *Book of Martyrs.*

gone home and relocated to avoid the ire of the believers who had lost loved ones to "the lie."

Frank Morison, a non-believing journalist, decided to disprove the resurrection. However, instead of refuting the resurrection, he became a strong believer in its historicity. He then wrote a classic book called *Who Moved The Stone?* which demonstrates the powerful evidence for the resurrection. Regarding the stolen body theory, Morison declares:

"I do not propose to devote any considerable amount of space to testing the historical accuracy of this charge, because the verdict has been anticipated by the most universal sense and feeling of mankind. So far as I know, there is not a single writer whose work is of critical value today who holds that there is even a case for discussion. We know these eleven men (the apostles) by their subsequent actions and writings. There is no trace of the daring sort of ringleader who would have the imagination to plan a coup like that and to carry it through without detection. Even if it had been possible and the disciples were the men who could do it, the subsequent history of Christianity would have been completely different. Sooner or later, someone who knew the facts would have been **unable to keep them hidden**. Further, no great moral structure like the early church, characterized as it was by life–long persecution and personal suffering, could have reared it's head on a statement that every one of the disciples knew to be a lie. Whatever the explanation for the empty tomb, we may be certain that it was not the disciples who stole the body."[1]

---

[1] *Who Moved the Stone?*, Frank Morison, pg. 89.

The Search For Messiah

Did Joseph of Arimathea Move the Body?

"Joseph of Arimathea, a prominent council member, who was himself waiting for the kingdom of God, coming and taking courage, went in to Pilate and asked for the body of Jesus." (Mark 15:43)

Joseph of Arimathea was a rich man, a member of the council of the Sanhedrin and a secret disciple of Jesus of Nazareth.[1] After the crucifixion, Joseph obtained the body by permission of Pontius Pilate, and buried Jesus in his new family tomb. According to some scholars, Joseph came to the tomb sometime between midnight and sunrise on Sunday, broke the Roman seal, then moved the stone and took the body to a more permanent resting place.

A close examination of this theory, however, reveals a number of inconsistencies.

Joseph of Arimathea was a member of the Sanhedrin and, therefore, could have obtained permission from the Jewish ruling council and the Romans to legitimately move the body at any hour he wished. So it is quite illogical to propose that a member of the Jewish government would secretly, in the middle of the night, try to move a body when he could have more easily accomplished this during the light of day.

What motivation would Joseph of Arimathea have for moving the body? If Joseph was a disciple, then all the arguments that we apply to the disciples stealing the body would apply to him. On the other hand, if he was a loyal Pharisee, why would a member of a group that despised Jesus be willing to risk ruination of his career by making such a stupid move?

---

[1]Matthew 27:57.

Furthermore, if Joseph of Arimathea was a loyal Pharisee, once the rumor of the resurrection came out, he could have easily produced the body and Christianity would have died on the spot.

On the other hand, if Joseph of Arimathea had made a perfectly legitimate removal of the body (say to avoid a popular uprising) then we know that other people had to assist him. In order to move a one to two ton stone and carry the body to another location, he would need at least three or four helpers, all of whom would have known the location of the body. These individuals could have provided the information and engendered great favor in the eyes of the council. For these reasons, the theory carries little weight and leaves the skeptic in want of a better scheme.

Did the Authorities Move the Body?

The first century Church was a thorn in the side of the Sanhedrin as well as the Roman Empire. Consequently, the early Christians were initially persecuted by the Sanhedrin and eventually by the Romans themselves. Despite this fact, some have actually proposed that the authorities of either Jerusalem or Rome moved the body of Jesus.

We know from the Gospels that the Temple priests wanted the tomb protected because of the rumor that Jesus was going to rise on the third day.[1] The members of the Sanhedrin recognized that a rumor of a risen Jesus would be even more harmful than a living Jesus. Therefore, they had a strong incentive to assure that the story of the resurrection did not get started.

The Romans also found Christianity disruptive to the empire. The spread of Christianity was harmful to the trade

---

[1]Matthew 27:63.

of idol production and the practice of Caesar worship. Consequently, they too had a strong incentive to prevent the spread of the resurrection story.

If the Roman or Jewish authorities did move the body for security reasons, then they knew its location. Such an operation, if it did occur, would have been done *specifically* to prevent the disciples from moving the body and declaring that Jesus rose. Therefore, when the disciples found the empty tomb and began to declare that Jesus had risen, the authorities needed only to produce the body. The disciples would have simply gone home, their hopes destroyed and the last three years of their lives wasted.

The skeptic will need to do better than this if a natural explanation for the empty tomb is to prevail.

The Swoon Theory

In the nineteenth century a German rationalist named Venturini developed the idea that Jesus did not die on the cross. Venturini proposed that Jesus simply fainted, or swooned, and was taken down from the cross alive, only to revive in the cold dark tomb. After awakening he unwrapped himself, moved a one to two ton stone, slipped by the Roman soldiers, returned to his disciples and convinced them that he had been resurrected.

From a medical, as well as a logical point of view, this is the least rational of all. This theory virtually ignores the character of the wounds that a crucifixion victim received.

We know from Roman history that victims of crucifixion were routinely beaten with a Roman cat-o'-nine-tails as many as forty times before the actual crucifixion. This device was a whip with long leather strips in which were imbedded glass, stone and lead chips. The whip had the effect of tearing off the skin and exposing the subcutaneous fat and muscle layers. Such a wound would result in the loss of large quantities of blood and fluid. If skin grafting and antibiotics are not immediately administered, such a wound would result in infection, dehydration and death within a two to three days. Obviously, no such treatment was available to Jesus. The New Testament account does not tell us how many stripes Jesus received from the Roman whip. However, there is no reason to expect that Jesus received anything less than a customary whipping. With the whipping injuries alone, Jesus would have been so weak that moving the stone would have been virtually impossible. The beating from a cat-o'-nine-tails by itself caused many people to die.

The practice of crucifixion was commonplace in the Roman empire. The Romans had perfected this form of capital punishment and were experts at recognizing death. Archaeological discoveries have revealed that metal spikes as long as nine inches were driven through the wrists and midfoot areas of the victim. These spikes would most likely sever the main artery to the foot (the dorsal pedal artery) resulting in even more loss of blood than caused by the cat-o'-nine-tails. The hands of the individual would be paralyzed from the severing of the median nerve, the main nerve to the hand.

After six hours of hanging on the cross, Jesus would have experienced massive blood loss. Consequently, he would have been severely dehydrated and would have probably developed pulmonary edema, a condition in which the lungs become congested with excess fluid. This is a catastrophic combination. The dehydration, coupled with pulmonary edema, rapidly sets into motion a cascade of multi-organ failure (that is, a total shutdown of kidney, liver, intestinal and cardiac blood flow), resulting in rapid development of respiratory failure, cardiac arrest and death.

Finally, at the end of the crucifixion, a Roman soldier thrust a spear into the side of Jesus, resulting in the drainage of blood and water. This is an indicator that Jesus had probably developed a pericardial effusion, a condition in which the pericardial sac around the heart fills with water, leading to heart failure and death.

If these very same injuries were to happen to a person on the front porch of a major university medical center, with a trauma team on standby, and even if surgery were initiated within six minutes, the victim would still almost certainly die. The sword wound through the side is so catastrophic that the loss of blood from this injury alone would result in brain death within minutes.

To propose and argue that a person who had suffered such wounds could revive, move a huge stone and get by the Roman guards, is incomprehensible to any thinking person.

Truly, the verdict of history and the facts of medical science affirm that Jesus died on a Roman cross.

The Women Went to the Wrong Tomb?

We know from the New Testament accounts that the first visitors to the tomb was a small band of women, disciples of Jesus. Some skeptics propose that after going to the wrong tomb and discovering it empty they returned to the men and declared that Jesus had risen. Proponents of this theory claim that the early morning darkness and the emotional state of the women were factors that contributed to the mistaken tomb.

Even a cursory review of this theory reveals a number of serious flaws. As we have seen, a typical Roman guard consisted of sixteen men, in full military uniform. If nothing else would tip off this group that they had found the tomb of Jesus, the presence of sixteen Roman soldiers in front of the tomb would have certainly been a clue! The women knew that there were soldiers at the tomb and would have known that an unguarded tomb was not the place where Jesus lay.

Secondly, once the rumor of the resurrection got started, the Romans could have produced the body. Rumor over!

The New Testament tells us that the Sanhedrin recognized the physical emptiness of the tomb and explained that the disciples had stolen the body. For the first several hundred years of the church, *the fact of the physical emptiness of the tomb was not doubted.* The stolen body theory was proposed *because there was* an empty tomb that had to be explained.

Finally, the proposal that the women never went to the tomb is incapable of explaining the behavior of the apostles and the martyrs of the early church.

As we look at the verdict of history, it is clear that there was no doubt in the minds of the disciples that Jesus died, that he was put in a tomb and that three days later he rose from the dead.

This conclusion is inescapable. It was the belief in the resurrection that drove the early Christians to incredible commitment and prepared them for unbelievable persecution. Any natural explanation for the empty tomb that is to be seriously considered must explain the commitment to servanthood and suffering among the early church and especially the people who met Jesus face to face.

To propose and argue that the early church, especially the apostles, were no different than the martyrs of any religious, social or political cause is simply not a fair comparison. The very early Christians (especially the twelve) were in a position to know the truth. Any secret conspiracy, any hidden body, any fact that would refute the resurrection would have been known by those men. When we look at the character of the early church, its rapid spread and the price Christians paid to follow Jesus, we recognize that something incredible must have occurred to engender this degree of devotion and sacrifice. Surely, an unsubstantiated claim by the women, a stolen or misplaced body, or a critically injured, severely weakened anemic Jesus, would not result in such devotion. Finally, the idea that Jesus' life, miracles and resurrection were only legends is totally and absolutely incapable of explaining the sacrificial lives and deaths by martyrdom of the early believers in Jesus' resurrection.

A resurrected Jesus does explain it all.

The Verdict is In!

In the last few centuries a number of leading lawyers have been challenged by students, peers or friends to evaluate the historical evidence for the resurrection. Using the accepted methods of legal and historical investigation, the resurrection of Jesus Christ has been declared by many to be an historical fact.

Sir Edward Clark, a former attorney for King's Court, stated regarding the legal and historical evidence for the resurrection:

"As a lawyer I have made a prolonged study of the
evidences for the events of the first Easter Day. To
me the evidence is conclusive, and over and over again
in the High Court I have secured the verdict on
evidence not nearly so compelling...The Gospel
evidence for the resurrection is of this class and, as a
lawyer, I accept it unreservedly as the testimony of
truthful men to facts they were able to substantiate."[1]

Regarding the conspiracy theory, former White House
counsel under Richard Nixon, Charles Colson, states:

"Take it from one who was inside the Watergate web
looking out, who saw firsthand how vulnerable a
cover-up is: Nothing less than a witness as awesome as
the resurrected Christ could have caused those men to
maintain to their dying whispers that Jesus is alive and
Lord." Charles Colson[2]

Charles Colson was one of the men in the Nixon
administration who went to prison because of the
Watergate cover-up of 1972. He saw firsthand how a
conspiracy breaks down when personal safety or position
is threatened. Within a day of its onset, the Watergate
cover-up began to unravel due to the mere threat of prison.
Immediately, finger pointing began as the parties scrambled
for position in order to get less prison time. Colson points
out that with the threat of torture and death hanging over
the heads of the disciples, no conspiracy could stand,
especially when recanting meant freedom. After the
Watergate scandal Colson examined the historical evidence
for Jesus, the early church and the resurrection of Jesus
Christ. Applying the methods of legal-historical

---

[1]Cited in *Leading Lawyers Look at the Resurrection*, Clifford, Appendix I,
Albatross Books, Claremont, CA, 1991.
[2]*Loving God*, Charles Colson, Marshalls, 1984, pg. 69.

investigation, Charles Colson became convinced of the deity of Christ and his bodily resurrection.[1]

Simon Greenleaf, born in 1783, is one of the most respected attorneys in the history of the American legal system. His book *A Treatise on the Law of Evidence* was a standard textbook for decades in law schools around the country. Later in his life he extensively examined historical evidence for the trial, death and resurrection of Jesus Christ. He concludes in his book that the resurrection of Jesus Christ is perhaps the most documented event in the history of mankind.[2]

When the evidence is examined in a fair and impartial manner, with pre-conceived notions aside, the verdict of history, sifted through the crucible of the legal-historical method, is conclusive. Something awesome, something radical, something life–changing, something supernatural happened in the lives of the twelve disciples of Jesus. That event was nothing less than the bodily resurrection of Jesus of Nazareth from the dead!

---

[1]See *Born Again*, Charles Colson.
[2]*The Testimony of the Evangelists Examined by the Rules of Evidence Administered in the Courts of Justice*, Simon Greenleaf, Baker, reprinted 1984.

CHAPTER 11

THE REJECTION OF JESUS CHRIST

"And Simon Peter answered and said, 'You are the Christ, the Son of the living God.'" (Matthew 16:16)

This declaration by Peter is a statement of faith. According to Jesus, this faith was given to him from the Father in heaven. Immediately prior to his death and after many years of reflecting on the life, ministry and meaning of Jesus, Peter stated:

> **"For we have not followed cunningly devised fables when we made known unto you the power and coming of our Lord Jesus Christ**, but were eyewitnesses of his majesty. For he received from God the Father honor and glory when there came such a voice to him from the Excellent Glory: 'This is My beloved Son, in whom I am well pleased.' And this voice which came from heaven we heard when we were with him on the holy mount. **We have also a more sure word of prophecy**; where unto ye do well ye take heed, as unto a light that shineth in a dark place, until the day dawn, and the day star arise in your hearts." (2 Peter 1:16-19 KJV)

After more than thirty years of telling people that he was an eyewitness to the "power and coming" of Jesus, Peter knew that many people found the story of this carpenter from Nazareth too good to be true, too incredible to accept. Consequently, he knew that many would attempt to explain it away as a myth or a "cunningly devised fable." So Peter essentially declares, "If you don't want to take my word for it then, we have also a more sure word of prophecy."

Here Peter appeals to the Messianic prophecies of the Tanakh, or Old Testament, and claims that the life, ministry and destiny of the Messiah, as spelled out in those prophecies, was fulfilled in the very life of Jesus Christ.

If this is so, if Jesus did fulfill so many Messianic prophecies, why then did the majority of the Jewish leadership reject him, while at the same time Peter and tens of thousands of first century Jews embraced and accepted Jesus as the very fulfillment of those prophecies?

Why have the rabbis so dramatically changed their views on those very same prophecies over the past 1900 years?

Finally, what difference does it make if Jesus is the Messiah?

The Rejection of Jesus

In this book we have examined only a small number of the hundreds of Messianic prophecies in the Tanakh. Nevertheless, we have been able to extract a fairly complete portrait of the Messiah's character, lineage, mission and destiny according to the ancient rabbis. We have found a number of very specific requirements that any Messianic candidate must fulfill in order to be taken seriously. And we have been able to support this portrait with the writings of ancient rabbis, men who were among the most respected teachers of their time. We will refer to this scripturally established portrait as the "biblical view."

We have seen that various rabbis of the last 2300 years believed the Messiah was an eternal being who would be the Son of God, born of a virgin, a miracle worker of the line of David, in the city of Bethlehem. Yet he would be mocked, despised and rejected. He would have his hands and feet pierced and die for the sins of the people. And we have found evidence from the Bible that the Messiah would be a physical manifestation of God.

According to the Tanakh, the Messiah was to come to the Second Temple and after his coming, that very same temple would be destroyed. After the Second Temple was destroyed, we find a number of rabbis expressing their dismay that the Messiah had not come! They attribute this failure to the sins of the nation of Israel.

Is our biblical portrait of Messiah fulfilled in Jesus? The answer, according to the people who were eyewitnesses to his life, the people who were willing to suffer horribly for their faith is an unequivocal yes! Jesus of Nazareth fulfilled the biblical view of the Messiah!

Why then, did the Sanhedrin reject him?

Earlier, in our discussion of the mood of first century Israel, we saw that while they were under the yoke of Roman oppression, a popular view of the Messiah had developed. Because of centuries of suffering under the yoke of foreigners, they began to yearn for the glorious, victorious Messiah, the one who would come in the clouds as "the Son of Man" to establish the everlasting Kingdom of God. This Messiah would rule on the throne of David forever. However, this one-sided view was based more on the hopes of the people, rather than the more complete biblical view so vividly painted by the prophets.

This popular view of the Messiah was not, however, totally void of a biblical basis. This Messiah was essentially the fulfillment of the ruling and reigning "vein" of prophecy. Those prophecies that spoke of the glorious ruling of the Messiah were extracted and embraced. Those that spoke of a suffering servant were placed on the back burner, to be fulfilled at another time, perhaps even by another individual. This dichotomy led to the two Messiah theory, a theory with not a shred of biblical support.

Despite their recognition of the suffering servant vein of prophecy, they were not expecting this part of the picture to be fulfilled when the Messiah came. In the minds of the first century Jews, a humble, lowly, suffering servant was the last thing they wanted in a Messiah.

The Jews of the first century were, in effect, expecting the *second coming* of the Messiah first!

It was this popular view of the Messiah that Jesus did not fulfill. Jesus of Nazareth was of the lineage of David, born of a virgin in Bethlehem, and based on biblical chronological indicators, he came at the expected time! Yet because he presented the image of a lowly servant, one who rode into Jerusalem on a donkey, one who was very critical of the Jewish leadership, he was rejected by the majority of the people.

The rejection was something that Jesus himself foretold over and over to his disciples. However, when we read their response we see an incredible lack of biblical and spiritual understanding on this issue. It is quite clear that the disciples were also victims of this popular view of the Messiah. In perhaps the clearest example of this lack of understanding we read:

> "From that time Jesus began to show to his disciples that he must go to Jerusalem, and suffer many things from the elders and chief priests and scribes, and be killed, and be raised again the third day. Then Peter took him aside and began to rebuke him, saying, 'Far be it from You, Lord; this shall not happen to You!' But he turned and said to Peter, 'Get behind Me, Satan! You are an offense to Me, for you are not mindful of the things of God, **but the things of men.**' " (Matthew 16:21-23)

This discourse took place after Peter's declaration that Jesus was the Christ, the Son of the Living God. Nevertheless, only moments later we see Peter demonstrating his one-sided, popular view of the Messiah. The response of Jesus must have startled Peter. Not only did he attribute the words of Peter to Satan but Jesus stated that Peter's one-sided view of the Messiah was "not mindful of the things of God, but the things of men." Jesus was declaring that Peter's one sided Messianic view was not of God but of men!

On another occasion Jesus spoke to all twelve disciples about his coming rejection and death and again their lack of understanding came through:

> "Then he took the twelve aside and said to them, 'Behold, we are going up to Jerusalem, and all things that are written by the prophets concerning the Son of Man will be accomplished. For he will be delivered to the gentiles and will be mocked and insulted and spit upon. And they will scourge him and put him to death. And the third day he will rise again.' But they understood none of these things; this saying was hidden from them, and they did not know the things which were spoken." (Luke 18:31)

The rejection of this miracle worker was incomprehensible to the twelve men who had seen so much good done by him. On many occasions the disciples demonstrated their expectation that Jesus was to set up his kingdom immediately. His teachings and miracles were enough to convince them that Jesus was indeed the Messiah, the Son of God. However, they too were expecting a Messiah who would immediately usher in the ruling and reigning vein of prophecy. Consequently, when Jesus himself told them bluntly that he must suffer, be put to death and rise on the third day, they were so blinded by the popular view of the Messiah that his message didn't sink in.

If the understanding that the Messiah was to suffer and die was so far from the consciousness of the men who loved and honored Jesus, how much farther away was this knowledge from the minds of men who hated and despised him? When the stinging criticism from Jesus pierced the hearts of the scribes and Pharisees, they discounted his many miracles and great following. Jesus' rejection of their superficial spirituality encouraged them to embrace the popular view and reject him as the Messiah. To them Jesus just didn't add up. They must have thought, "Surely, we, the leaders of Judaism, would recognize the Messiah when he comes." And yet, despite Jesus' uncanny fulfillment of prophecy and his miraculous ministry, they rejected him.

It Pleased the Lord to Bruise Him!

Thus far we have looked at the rejection of Jesus purely from a man–centered point of view. In our limited, four dimensional minds, we cannot hope to understand the deepest methods and purposes of God. But there are elements of God's plan that we can understand. And even a casual understanding of the Tanakh reveals that the atoning death of the Messiah has been a part of God's plan from before the beginning of time!

The main purpose of the Bible is to reveal to man the purposes and ways of God. If importance can be measured by volume, then the most important purpose of the Bible is to reveal the way by which man can be reconciled or justified in the sight of God. In the Old Testament, in the book of Leviticus we find the laws regarding animal sacrifice as an atonement for sins.

> "'For the life of the flesh is in the blood, and I have given it to you upon the altar to make atonement for your souls; for it is the blood that makes atonement for the soul.'" (Leviticus 17:11)

In order to cover or atone for one's sins or transgressions individuals were required to go to the Temple and offer an unspotted, unblemished animal on a regular basis. The blood of the animal was sprinkled on the mercy seat of the Ark of the Covenant and provided a covering for a person's sins. This sacrificial system, however, offered only temporary atonement, or covering, for sins. Consequently, each time a person sinned, it was necessary to atone or cover the sin with such a sacrifice.

On a national level, each year on the Day of Atonement the High Priest was required to go into the Holy of Holies and offer a sacrifice for the nation of Israel. After this sacrifice, a red ribbon was tied around the neck of a goat (called the scapegoat) and it was released into the wilderness. The goat was followed for many days and when the red ribbon turned white, it was a sign that the sins of the nation were forgiven.

This tradition probably developed as a result of this prophecy:

> "'Come now, and let us reason together,' says the LORD, 'Though your sins are like scarlet, they shall be

as white as snow; though they are red like crimson, they shall be as wool.'" (Isaiah 1:18)

The writer of the book of Hebrews points out that the sacrificial system, though efficacious for a time, provided only a temporary covering for sins:

"For the law, having a shadow of the good things to come, and not the very image of the things, can never with these same sacrifices, which they offer continually year by year, make those who approach perfect. For then would they not have ceased to be offered? For the worshipers, once purged, would have had no more consciousness of sins. But in those sacrifices there is a reminder of sins every year. For it is not possible that the blood of bulls and goats could take away sins." (Hebrews 10:1)

The Levitical sacrificial system only covered over a person's sins. The writer of the book of Hebrews points out that such sacrifices did not take away a man's sins, but were in fact a continual reminder of one's sinfulness. If such sacrifices could permanently justify a man in the sight of God then those sacrifices would have to be done but once.

Because of the temporary nature of the sacrificial system there needed to be something more permanent and efficacious that could take away a man's sins, something that the writer of Hebrews says cannot be accomplished by the blood of bulls and goats.

The Daysman

In the book of Job we read of the righteousness and suffering of Job, a man whom God called "a whole-hearted man and an upright man, one that feareth God and shunneth evil."[1] In the story of Job we read that God allowed Satan to afflict Job with the loss of his personal possessions, his health and even the loss of his family. When Job's friends saw his predicament they told him that these things had occurred because he had sinned and needed to get right with God.

Job knew that he, being a man, was by nature sinful, and agreed that a righteous standing before God was something good and necessary. However, he was unaware of any specific sin that he had done to bring on his plight. Nevertheless, he answers:

> "Truly I know it is so, but how can a man be righteous before God?" (Job 9:2)

Job recognized the incredible gulf between man and God, a gulf that could not be spanned by good works. But in his despair he recognized there was no mediator to bridge that gap and justify him in the sight of God, so he cried out:

> "Nor is there any daysman [mediator] between us, that might lay his hand upon us both." (Job 9:33 KJV)

What Job did not know was that God had a plan. The sacrificial system of covering the sins of man with the blood of animals was only a shadow of things to come. It did not wipe the slate clean. It only covered the sin. God had something wonderful and permanent planned for the removal of sin. No longer would sin be simply covered, it would be wiped clean. God, through the prophet Jeremiah, stated:

> " 'Behold, the days are coming,' says the LORD, **'when I will make a new covenant with the**

---

[1]Job 1:8, JPS, 1917.

house of Israel and with the house of Judah; not according to the covenant that I made with their fathers in the day that I took them by the hand to bring them out of the land of Egypt, My covenant which they broke, though I was a husband to them,' says the LORD. 'But this is the covenant that I will make with the house of Israel: After those days, says the LORD, **I will put My law in their minds, and write it on their hearts; and I will be their God, and they shall be My people.**'" (Jeremiah 31:31-33)

When we examine the Messianic suffering servant vein of prophecies, we find some startling and unexpected aspects of his mission. We discover that this promised deliverer would fulfill an undeniable role of the daysman or mediator between God and man. In his role as the mediator the Messiah justifies the sinner in the sight of God making atonement for our sins.

In the Levitical sacrificial system, only an unblemished animal could be used in the process of covering sins. Consequently, for the Messiah to act as mediator and make atonement for sins, he must be unblemished, free from sin himself. According to these verses, all men have sinned and are, therefore, "blemished" by their sin.

I Kings 8:46 says: "For *when they sin against you—for there is no one who does not sin...*"

Ecclesiastes 7:20 says: "For *there is not a just man on earth who does good and does not sin.*"

Sinless perfection is something no mere mortal has ever accomplished.

However, the fact that the Messiah is free of sin was clearly believed by at least some ancient rabbis. We noted earlier a quote from Psalter of Solomon (written by an unknown Jewish source around 50 B.C.E.). Referring to Isaiah 9:6-7 the writer states of the Messiah, *"He is pure from sin."*

Also, in the book of Isaiah itself, in an undeniable Messianic verse, we read of the sinlessness of the Messiah:

"And they made his grave with the wicked; but with the rich at his death, because he had done no violence, nor was any deceit in his mouth." (Isaiah 53:9)

Consequently, since the Messiah is without "spot or blemish," he is able and worthy to take on the role of mediator or daysman.

How the Messiah accomplishes his role as mediator is astonishing and unexpected. He takes on the role of the sacrificial offering itself. Through his death Messiah accomplishes atonement of sins, the mediation between man and God and the fulfillment of the suffering servant "vein" of prophecy.

The Messiah–The Lamb of God

Isaiah, inspired of God, spoke of the Messiah as a sacrificial lamb:

"He was oppressed and he was afflicted, yet he opened not his mouth; he was led as a lamb to the slaughter, and as a sheep before its shearers is silent, so he opened not his mouth." (Isaiah 53:7)

Here, in another undeniable Messianic passage, we see the sacrificial role of the Messiah expressed in the idiom of a lamb led to slaughter. When John the Baptist saw Jesus of Nazareth he declared that Jesus was not only the sacrificial Lamb of God, but that through his sacrifice the sins of the world would be completely removed and not simply covered.

> "The next day John saw Jesus coming toward him, and said, 'Behold! The Lamb of God who takes away the sin of the world!' " (John 1:29)

Finally, in the following verses, in the clearest possible terms, we read that God accepted the atoning death of the Messiah.

> "All we like sheep have gone astray; we have turned, every one, to his own way; and **the LORD has laid on him the iniquity of us all**...He was taken from prison and from judgment, and who will declare his generation? **For he was cut off from the land of the living; for the transgressions of My people he was stricken... Yet it pleased the LORD to bruise him; he has put him to grief.** When You make his soul an offering for sin, he shall see his seed, he shall prolong his days, and the pleasure of the LORD shall prosper in his hand. He shall see the travail of his soul, and be satisfied. By his knowledge **My righteous Servant shall justify many, for he shall bear their iniquities.** Therefore I will divide him a portion with the great, and he shall divide the spoil with the strong, **because he poured out his soul unto death, and he was numbered with the transgressors, and he bore the sin of many, and made intercession for the transgressors.**" (Isaiah 53:6,8,10-12)

As we have noted earlier, the ancient rabbis recognized these verses as an *unmistakable* reference to the Messiah. In these verses we find the *pleasure* of God expressed because his people are justified (made righteous in his sight) through the rejection, bruising and sacrificial, substitutionary death of the Messiah. The One born of a virgin, who would be called the Mighty God, the Prince of

Peace, the everlasting Father and Immanuel, our mediator, Job's "daysman!"

The Messianic message of scripture is that God himself became a man in the person of the Messiah, lived the perfect life, died as a spotless lamb led to slaughter and bridged the enormous gulf between sinful man and the eternal perfect God. No mere animal sacrifice, no mere mortal could span such a gulf. The gap needed to be spanned by a perfect sacrifice, something that could only be accomplished by the perfection found within God himself.

Overwhelmed by the incredible plan of God, the Apostle John exclaimed:

"Behold what manner of love the Father has bestowed on us, that we should be called children of God!" (1 John 3:1)

Reflecting on the sacrificial, substitutionary death of Jesus, the spotless Lamb of God, the Apostle Peter wrote:

"Knowing that you were not redeemed with corruptible things, like silver or gold, from your aimless conduct received by tradition from your fathers, but with the precious blood of Christ, as of a lamb without blemish and without spot." (1 Peter 1:18-19)

The incredible paradox of Christianity is that Jesus Christ *had* to die in order to accomplish the atonement of our sins. And by doing so, Jesus is now perfectly situated to fulfill the second vein of prophecy at his second coming, a role that he himself declared that he would fulfill when he comes again.

In the book of Daniel we are given a picture of the arrival of the Messiah in his glory rather than humility:

"I was watching in the night visions, and behold, One like the Son of Man, coming with the clouds of heaven! He came to the Ancient of Days, and they brought him near before him." (Daniel 7:13)

When Jesus of Nazareth declared to his disciples the signs that would precede his second coming, he finished with these words:

"Then the sign of the Son of Man will appear in heaven, and then all the tribes of the earth will mourn, and they will see the Son of Man coming on the clouds of heaven with power and great glory." (Matthew 24:30)

These words parallel exactly the words of Daniel 7:13.

The Levitical System Removed

With the perfect sacrifice accomplished in the spotless lamb of God, we find that within a generation the Levitical system of animal sacrifice was abolished. In the year 70 C.E., the Roman general Titus sacked Jerusalem, destroyed the Second Temple, killed millions of Jews in the process and dispersed the remaining remnant into foreign territories. With the city of Jerusalem and the temple destroyed, the Levitical system of animal sacrifice was no longer being practiced. However, the Babylonian Talmud hints that the system had lost its efficacy nearly forty years earlier.

As we saw earlier, in the days of the Second Temple there was a custom to fasten a red-colored strip of wool to the head of a goat which was to be sent away on the Day of Atonement. When this red ribbon became white, it was a sign that God had forgiven Israel's sins. In one of the most astonishing portions of the Babylonian Talmud we find the statement that about:

"...forty years before the Second Temple was destroyed...the red wool did not become white! " [1]

The same passage informs us that at that time the gates of the Temple swung open on their own accord!

According to this portion of the Talmud, these events were indicators to the ancient rabbis *that the sins of Israel were not being forgiven anymore and the Temple would soon be destroyed!*[2]

The Levitical system of animal sacrifice was no longer efficacious and no longer necessary. The perfect sacrifice had been made.

The God–given sign which was an indicator that the sins of the people had been forgiven was removed around the year 30 C.E! This corresponds to the very time period when Jesus of Nazareth was sacrificed as the Lamb of God to take away the sins of the world.

The fact that the removal of this sign was recorded in the Talmud by men who were antagonistic to the message of Christianity, is nothing less than astonishing.

Since the destruction of the Second Temple, the rabbis have developed a system of "good works" to atone or balance out one's sins. Faced with the dilemma of no temple in which to perform animal sacrifices, the rabbis needed to come up with some system by which an observant Jew could obtain a righteous standing before God. Consequently, the rabbis of the Talmudic and Midrashic period began to promote the idea that a sin could

---

[1] Babylonian Talmud, Yoma chapter 39b.
[2] Adapted from *The Messianic Hope*, Arthur Kac, pg. 227.

be erased or balanced out by a good deed. Consequently, a tradition developed that as long as one's good deeds outnumbered the bad, then a person would be accounted as justified or righteous in the sight of God. Each year, as the Day of Atonement approaches, Jews are admonished to examine themselves and determine whether their good deeds outweigh their bad. If not, then a flurry of good deeds at the end of the year should take care of the sin problem.

Although on the surface this tradition of good works outweighing the bad seems reasonable, there is not a shred of biblical support for its validity. In fact, the Tanakh even mocks the concept.

> "But we are all like an unclean thing, **and all our righteousnesses are like filthy rags;** we all fade as a leaf, and our iniquities, like the wind, have taken us away." (Isaiah 64:6)

The word translated as "filthy rags" is literally "used menstrual cloths." Apparently the translators felt that the public couldn't handle such a comparison. God, however, wanted us to have a vivid picture of how he views our self-attained righteousness.

Surely, such a righteousness cannot justify us in the sight of God.

The Offense of the Cross

> "'For My thoughts are not your thoughts, nor are your ways My ways,' says the LORD." (Isaiah 55:8)

Some of you may be offended, as I was, by the message of Jesus. To think that the shed blood of a Jewish carpenter would be the way by which God would atone for the sins of man seems insulting and ridiculous to many, especially to the modern observant Jew. Interestingly, this reaction was anticipated by God. He realized that many in the nation of Israel would stumble spiritually and reject the Messiah when he came. This is expressed in the Messianic verse:

> "He will be as a sanctuary, but a stone of stumbling and a rock of offense to both the houses of Israel, as a trap and a snare to the inhabitants of Jerusalem." (Isaiah 8:14)

Jesus also recognized that many would be offended by his exclusive claim of being *the way* of salvation. Consequently, he encouraged his disciples to remain steadfast in their faith in him and to:

> "Enter by the narrow gate; for wide is the gate and broad is the way that leads to destruction, and there are many who go in by it. Because narrow is the gate and difficult is the way which leads to life, and there are few who find it." (Matthew 7:13-14)

Paul the Apostle, one of the Pharisees that *did* become a believer in the Messiahship of Jesus, stated this regarding the apparent foolishness of the substitutionary death of the Messiah:

> **"For the message of the cross is foolishness to those who are perishing**, but to us who are being saved it is the power of God." (1 Corinthians 1:18)

Regarding the offense of the cross of Jesus Christ, Paul paraphrased Isaiah 28:16:

> "As it is written: 'Behold, I lay in Zion a stumbling stone and rock of offense and whoever believes on him will not be put to shame.' " (Romans 9:33)

If you are offended by the message of the sacrificial, substitutionary death of Jesus Christ, **it is also important to consider that your objection was anticipated by God, by Jesus himself and the Apostle Paul.**

Jesus' Promises to His Disciples

"Come to Me, all you who labor and are heavy laden, and I will give you rest. Take My yoke upon you and learn from Me, for I am gentle and lowly in heart, and you will find rest for your souls. For My yoke is easy and My burden is light." (Matthew 11:28-30)

The fact that Jesus anticipated his own rejection (as well as the rejection of his disciples) is in itself a powerful evidence for the truth of his Messianic claim. Normally when a religious crackpot comes around he will say things like, "Come to me and I will give you peace, joy, eternal life, prosperity. You will be popular and loved by many."

Jesus didn't say this. In addition to promising his followers joy, peace and eternal life, he also made some less appealing predictions for them.

"And you will be hated by all for My name's sake. But he who endures to the end will be saved." (Matthew 10:22)

"But before all these things, they will lay their hands on you and persecute you, delivering you up to the synagogues and prisons, and you will be brought before kings and rulers for My name's sake. But it will turn out for you as an occasion for testimony...You will be betrayed even by parents and brothers, relatives and friends; and they will send some of you to your death. And you will be hated by all for My name's sake."
(Luke 21:12-13, 16-17)

"If the world hates you, you know that it hated Me before it hated you." (John 15:18)

"Blessed are you when men hate you, and when they exclude you, and revile you and cast out your name as evil, for the Son of Man's sake. Rejoice in that day and leap for joy! For indeed your reward is great in heaven, for in like manner their fathers did to the prophets." (Luke 6:22 -23)

"Do you suppose that I came to give peace on earth? I tell you, not at all, but rather division. For from now on five in one house will be divided: three against two, and two against three...." (Luke 12:51-52)

Jesus was a campaign manager's nightmare! Political correctness was obviously not part of his ministry. But this points out an interesting piece of evidence for his Messiahship.

If Jesus knew that he wasn't the Messiah, and he was trying to gain a following for the purpose of proclaiming himself as the Messiah, then he would have never made such statements to his potential followers. But if he was the Messiah, the Son of the Living God, then it would be natural that he would tell them the truth and desire to prepare them for the rejection of their Christian message. So in making such claims to his disciples, he was, in effect, validating his status as Messiah. Jesus was to suffer and so would his followers.

You Shall Not Add to the Word

After the death and resurrection of Jesus, thousands of first century Jews came to a saving belief in the Messiahship of Jesus. One of the primary tools used in presenting Jesus as the Messiah was the use of Old Testament prophecy.

Apparently, however, rabbinical Judaism had had enough of these appeals to the Messianic prophecies in the Tanakh. During the Talmudic and Midrashic period, 200-1400 C.E., the interpretation of almost every Messianic prophecy began to change. The result is that the modern Messianic beliefs of Judaism are almost 180 degrees opposite of their ancient counterparts.

Instead of a Messiah who would be the supernatural Son of God, one born of a virgin, one who would raise the dead, heal the sick and yet be despised, rejected and apparently killed by some sort of piercing, modern rabbis await a Messiah who is just a man, with no supernatural traits at all. This belief is so contrary to the views of the ancient rabbis that it is almost impossible to imagine how the modern position could have evolved to the point where it is now.

We can only speculate what may have been the motivating force that caused the rabbis to so dramatically change their interpretation of Messianic prophecy.

If the motivating force was the effective use of prophecy as an evangelistic tool by Christians, then this is a great tragedy and a disservice to the Jewish people. If the rabbis of the past nineteen centuries were so confident in their rejection of Jesus of Nazareth as the Messiah, then they should have stuck to their guns and embraced the ancient rabbinical interpretations since the ancients clearly had a much greater knowledge of the Hebrew language and customs than do the modern rabbis.

In most cases the rabbis of the Midrashim simply changed the interpretation of the many Messianic prophecies. However, in the case of Isaiah 53, the Ashkenazi Jews eliminated it from their Bible for centuries. Still other examples were more subtle. As we saw in the case of Psalm 22, it was the changing of a single letter from "karv" כארש (pierced) to the word "kari" כארי (like a lion).

Finally, in the case of Deuteronomy 32:43 it was the elimination of the phrase "let all the angels of God worship him," a possible reference to the Messiah. Now one might argue that these were just slips of the pen. However, to eliminate the entire text of Isaiah 53 and the first portion of Deuteronomy 32:43 would clearly take an act of malicious editorial license.

What does God say about tampering with his word?

"You shall not add to the word which I command you, **nor take anything from it**, that you may keep the commandments of the LORD your God which I command you." (Deuteronomy 4:2)

What is the penalty for disobeying God's command? In the times of the Tanakh it was no less than death!

When Messiah Comes Again

"The stone which the builders rejected has become the chief cornerstone." (Psalms 118:22)

In the prophecies of the suffering servant we encounter the negative response of the majority of the people at Messiah's first coming. He was despised and rejected. It is fascinating to me that this is exactly the response of the majority of people alive today to Jesus. However, God in his wisdom has left no stone unturned. Not only did he predict the response at the Messiah's first coming, he also predicted the response of the nation of Israel upon Messiah's second coming!

When the Messiah arrives, in this or a future generation, and when he is recognized by the nation of Israel, God says that:

> "... I will pour upon the house of David and upon the inhabitants of Jerusalem the Spirit of grace and supplication; then they will look on Me whom they have pierced; they will mourn for him as one mourns for his only son, and grieve for him as one grieves for a firstborn." (Zechariah 12:10)

Earlier we saw that the ancient rabbis believed this verse was a reference to the slaying of Messiah:

> "What is the cause of the mourning [of Zechariah 12:10]. It is well according to him who explains that **the cause is the slaying of Messiah, the son of Joseph,** since that well agrees with the Scriptural verse, **'And they shall look upon me because they have thrust him through, and they shall mourn for him as one mourneth for his only son.' "** (Talmud, Sukkah 52a)

Israel will weep when they see the One who was slain as a lamb to slaughter.

The lamb who had been slain was also seen by the Apostle John.

> "And I looked, and behold, in the midst of the throne and of the four living creatures, and in the midst of the elders, stood a Lamb as though it had been slain, having seven horns and seven eyes, which are the seven Spirits of God sent out into all the earth." (Revelation 5:6)

A friend of mine told me of a discussion he had with a rabbi recently. The rabbi told him that one of the first questions that he will ask the Messiah when he comes is, "Have you been here before?" I think if you have examined the evidence presented so far in this book, you can see that the Messiah's response will definitely be "YES!"

Have you been stumbled by the claims of Jesus? Have you made up your mind without considering the evidence? Have you decided not to decide regarding this carpenter from Nazareth? The decision you make about Jesus of Nazareth will affect your eternal destiny forever.

"Therefore, behold, I will again do a marvelous work among this people, a marvelous work and a wonder; for the wisdom of their wise men shall perish, and the understanding of their prudent men shall be hidden." (Isaiah 29:14)

NOTES

CHAPTER 12

THE CLAIMS OF CHRIST

by Chuck Smith

"Jesus said to him, 'I am the way, the truth, and the life.
No one comes to the Father except through Me.'"
(John 14:6)

Death is not the end of human existence. The Bible
states that it is appointed unto man once to die, and then
comes the judgment. After the judgment every person will
find himself forever in heaven or in hell. Your eternal
destiny will be determined by whether or not you believe
the claims of Jesus Christ.

In John 12:44 we read:

"Jesus cried and said, 'he that believes on Me, believes
not on Me, but on him that sent Me. He that sees Me,
sees him that sent Me. I am come as a light into the
world, that whosoever believes in Me should not abide
in darkness. If any man hears my words and believes
not, I judge him not, for I did not come to judge the
world, but to save the world. Whoever rejects Me and
receives not My words has one that judges him; the
word that I have spoken shall judge him in that last
day. For I have not spoken of Myself, but the Father
which sent Me, he commanded Me what I should say
and what I should speak. I know that his
commandment is life everlasting. I speak whatever the
Father said unto Me to speak.' "

Jesus: A Radical!

Let's look at the radical claims that Jesus has made concerning himself in these few verses.

1. Believing upon him was equivalent to believing the One who sent him, or upon the Father. Over and over, he avowed that God sent him.

2. To believe on him was equivalent to believing in God.

3. To see him was the same as seeing God.

4. He claimed to come as a light into the world.

5. Those who believe in him do not abide in darkness.

6. He stated that he came to save the world.

7. He claimed that those who do not believe in him will be judged by the word that he has spoken.

8. He claimed that his teaching did not originate with him, but that he spoke the words that the Father commanded him to speak.

9. He declared that his words are life everlasting.

These are the claims of Jesus. There is no denying the fact that they are quite radical. The extreme nature of Jesus' statements concerning himself presents every person with a choice to be made. We must either accept or reject his claims. We must either believe or disbelieve him. It is not an option to simply ignore or try to evade such radical statements. What Jesus said demands that we form an opinion, and our opinion will ultimately fall into one of two camps. He was either telling the truth or he was lying. He was either the Son of God and the greatest person who ever lived or he was a deceiver and a fraud. You may be more kind and say, "I believe that perhaps he believed those things, but he was deluded and if he were living today, he would probably be institutionalized." But the issue remains, are his claims true or false? Jesus is who he claimed to be or he isn't.

Jesus The Miracle Man

In the New Testament, we read of many signs that Jesus did to substantiate the claims that he was making. In the fourteenth chapter of John, Jesus reiterates some of these things that he has claimed here, but also adds a few more such as, "I am the Way, the Truth, and the Life, and no man can come to the Father except through Me"; "If you have seen Me, you have seen the Father"; and "Believe that I am in the Father and the Father is in Me, or else believe for the very work's sake." In other words, Jesus not only claimed to be God in human flesh, the perfect source of truth and the One who grants eternal life, but offered conclusive proof through the miraculous deeds or "works" he was doing. In the Gospel of John, Jesus said that John the Baptist bore witness of him, but that there was a greater witness than that of John. This greater witness was the works that the Father had given him to do. Among these authenticating signs was Jesus' power over the elements. He turned the water into wine, he walked on the water, and he calmed a raging storm by his word. He showed his power over disease for he healed the suffering with a touch. He cleansed those with leprosy. He caused the lame to walk, opened the eyes of the blind and even raised the dead. He called upon these works to verify that his teaching was true.

At another time when huge crowds had gathered around him, Jesus said, "A faithless and perverse generation seeks a sign, but no sign will be given, except that of the prophet Jonah. For as Jonah was three days and three nights in the belly of the whale, so shall the Son of man be three days and three nights in the heart of the earth." Thus his resurrection would constitute the basic sign to an unbelieving world that he was all that he claimed to be.

When Jesus cleansed the temple of the money changers, he was asked by the Jews for a sign of authority to do what he had done. His response was, "Destroy this temple, and in three days I will rebuild it." John tells us that he was referring to his own body as a temple, thus the resurrection from the grave three days after his death would constitute the ultimate sign.

Many Infallible Proofs

In Acts 1:3 we read that Jesus showed himself alive after his death by "many infallible proofs." The resurrection of Jesus from the dead is one of the most factually verifiable events in history. It is confirmed by the testimony of many eyewitnesses such as Mary, Peter, the other apostles and more than 500 people at one time. If there is any validity to our system of jurisprudence, which establishes fact on the basis of eyewitness testimony, then the resurrection must be accepted as fact. "But," you may argue, "there was no cross examination of the witnesses." Are you certain of that? Let it be noted that the vast majority of these witnesses were violently killed for their testimony, and none recanted, though doing so could have spared their lives. (For more information see Foxe's *Book of Martyrs.*) So many gave their lives for what they had seen and heard that the Greek word "martus" (which meant one who bore legal testimony) came to mean those who suffered death for the Christian witness.

But along with his miraculous works and his historical resurrection from the dead, we have to also take into consideration the multiplied prophecies concerning the Messiah that Jesus fulfilled. Throughout the Old Testament, there were more than 300 predictions concerning the Messiah that were fulfilled in the birth, life, death and resurrection of Christ. What would be the odds of one person fulfilling those prophecies by chance? The number is so astronomical, that it puts chance out of the picture.

The Odds

In his book *Science Speaks*, Peter Stoner estimates the odds of one person fulfilling just eight of these Messianic prophecies as being one in ten to the seventeenth power (1 in 10^{17})[1]. How overwhelming is this probability? Stoner illustrates this by supposing that we take ten to the seventeenth power silver dollars and lay them on the face of Texas. They will cover all of the state two feet deep. Now mark one of these silver dollars and stir the whole mass thoroughly, all over the state. Blindfold a man and tell him that he can travel as far as he wishes, but he must pick up one silver dollar and say this is the right one. What chance would he have of getting the right one? Just the same chance that the prophets would have had of writing these eight prophecies and having them come true in any one man, from their day to the present time. It is clear that chance had nothing to do with the fulfillment of these 300 predictions.

---

[1]*Science Speaks,* Stoner, Peter W, Chicago: Moody Press, 1963.

It is also important to note that the design spelled out in prophecy was far beyond any one person's ability to control. From the place of the Messiah's birth to the amount of money offered for his betrayal, we find factors that were out of any person's ability to arrange. Jesus could not by chance or by his own personal effort have fulfilled those 300 predictions. It had to be by God's design.

Peter lived in close association with Jesus for three years and was with him on some of the most momentous occasions of his ministry. Many times when the other disciples were excluded, Peter was brought in to see the special work of God. When they came to the house of Jairus, whose little daughter had died, Jesus put all of the people out. Yet he took Peter and John into the room that they might be witnesses of his power to bring her back to life. When he was in the area of Caesarea Philippi and was transfigured on the high mountain before his disciples, it was Peter, James and John who were selected by the Lord to witness the event. In his second epistle, Peter writes about this experience and describes Jesus with his raiment shining like the sun, and seeing that glory of the eternal God coming forth from him. He said, "We were not following cunningly devised fables when we declared to you the glory of the Lord." It wasn't some cunningly devised story. He said, "We were actual eye witnesses of his glory when we heard the voice of God there on the Mount." But even as significant as this experience was, Peter pointed to "the more sure word of prophecy" as the secure foundation of our faith.

When predictions are made about the future, there is a governing principle known as the Law of Compound Probabilities. This principle states that the more conditions placed on a prediction, the greater the chance that it will not come to pass.

Let us say that Newport Beach in California is shaken by an earthquake on an average of once every two years. If I should predict that there will be an earthquake in Newport this year, my chances are 1 in 2 of being right. If I said it will happen on June thirteenth, then there being 365 days in a year, the chances of it happening the thirteenth of June would be 1 in 365. If I said it would happen this year on June 13th, the chances would be 2 x 365 or 1 in 730. If I then declared it would happen this year, on June 13, at 2:05 in the afternoon, there being 1,440 minutes in a day, the likelihood of accuracy would then be 2 x 365 x 1,440 or 1 in 1,051,200. Now if I wanted to be very daring and say that the quake would strike at 2:05 and 15 seconds, I would increase the chances tremendously, for there are 86,400 seconds in a day x 1,051, 200 and thus the chances of it happening as predicted are 1 in 90,823,680,000. This is just considering four factors. If I added more factors to the prediction, such as magnitude, epicenter, and the money needed to repair the damage, until I had 300 conditions, can you imagine what the odds against such a prediction being fulfilled would be? If they all came to pass you would have to conclude that I was either a true prophet, or else had inside information. This is exactly the situation we face with the prophecies concerning Jesus. He fulfilled over 300 conditions prophesied of him. No wonder Peter called it the more sure word of prophecy!

Sufficient Proof

There is certainly sufficient evidence and proof that the claims of Jesus were true. If you do not believe these claims, it is not because they are unbelievable, or because they are lacking in evidence. You don't believe because you don't want to believe. Why would a person not want to believe the glorious claims of Jesus? He is claiming that he came to save you. He is claiming that his words will bring you everlasting life. But he is also declaring that if you don't believe, one day you will stand before God in judgment. He would not judge you, but you would be judged by the words that he spoke, because you didn't believe them. He said that he came that you might have life, and that more abundantly. Why would a person not want to believe that? Jesus loves us and died to save us from the penalty of sin, which is death. He loves us and died in our place that we might have eternal life. Why would a person not want to believe that? Many times a person doesn't want to believe because faith in Christ would require that they change their lifestyle. They are living after their selfish desires and they love their way of life. The commandments that Jesus gave are not pleasant for a person who wants to live after his fleshly lust. Jesus said if you would come after him, you should deny yourself and take up your cross and follow him. He condemned adultery, but many desire to have affairs. He condemned stealing, but many want to steal. He condemned immoral sexual expression, but many desire to throw off any and all moral restraints.

This world says, "Indulge yourself!" There is so much emphasis in the world today upon self indulgence. People don't like to hear that they have to deny what they may want at a given moment. Thus, they don't want to believe on Jesus because it would require a change of lifestyle. Jesus said that people will not come to the light because one of the characteristics of light is exposing that which is in darkness. The secret hidden things are covered by darkness. Thus he said they will not come to the light because their deeds are evil. They hate the light and don't want to be exposed by the light. Have you ever noticed how places like bars are kept purposefully dark? People there want to hide. They really don't want to be seen. They love the darkness rather the light because their deeds are evil. Jesus said that was the reason many will not believe in him.

"I'd Like to Believe But..."

If you do not believe in the claims of Jesus, I would be very interested in hearing the reasons why. Why don't you believe them? Some will say, "Well, I don't believe those things because if salvation was such a wonderful thing then everyone would be saved." That sounds rather logical, yet does that mean you don't believe in soap, because there are a lot of dirty people in the world? Would you like to make an argument that soap is of no value at all? Look at all the dirty people in the world. If soap was so good, why isn't everyone in the world clean?

Some have said they believed until God failed to answer their prayers. In fact, Ted Turner claims that at one time in his life he was a Christian. His sister was very sick when he was a boy and he prayed that God would heal her, but she died. After that incident, he no longer believed in God. There are many people like Ted Turner, who have been disappointed because God did not answer a particular prayer. When God did not answer, they concluded that he did not exist. Of course, God is not obligated to answer our every prayer. In reality, I would not want God to answer any prayer of mine that wasn't according to his will. I wouldn't want to force God to do something that he was reluctant to do. So often we think that God is like a Santa Claus that is suppose to respond to our every whim. To reject God because he didn't answer a prayer is as childish as saying, "Well if I can't be the chief of police, I'm not going to play with you anymore! I'm going home! If you don't do it my way, then you won't have me for a friend." This is at best an immature basis for a relationship.

Yet that is the kind of relationship many people try to have with God. "As long as God plays along with my wishes and my desires, I'll believe in him and I'll play along with the game. But let him cross me once and that's the end. I won't believe anymore. I'll take my marbles and go home."

A Rabbit Eats a Man's Faith

Ignorance can also be a factor in rejecting Christ. I heard of a man who said he believed in God and in the Bible until one day he read a section in Leviticus concerning the animals that were unclean to eat. It was telling the factors that determine whether a species was clean or unclean. Mentioned in this section was the hare (which he interpreted to be a rabbit) which according to the passage was a cud chewing animal. Believing that rabbits don't chew cud, he concluded that the Bible contained an error of fact and was therefore not trustworthy. So he quit believing in God after he read in the Bible that the rabbit chews the cud. Interestingly, a bit of research could of cleared up this problem.

Some Hebrew scholars question whether the word in this passage actually refers to a rabbit. The Hebrew word arnebeth (translated hare) is of uncertain derivation. Biologists have also come to the conclusion that rabbits do exhibit a behavior very similar to chewing cud. But the more important point is to note how easily some people will dismiss the entire message of Scripture based upon the misunderstanding of a relatively insignificant particular. Imagine what it would be like to stand before God on Judgment Day with this kind of attitude. "Well, I used to believe in You until I read in Your Bible that the rabbit chews the cud." Could you imagine hearing God reply, "That's not a hare. That's an arnebeth. It's not even in the rabbit family."

I have encountered many people who have tossed out their faith based upon some supposed contradiction or error they found in Scripture. Many of these problems can be avoided by understanding certain rules of biblical interpretation that we need to know and follow. First of all, let me say that I don't pretend to understand everything that is in the Bible. There are a lot of things in the Bible that I quite frankly will confess to you that I don't understand. If I were smarter, I might. However, if my interpretation of a passage is blatantly contradictory to another verse of scripture, that doesn't mean the scripture is wrong, only that my interpretation is wrong. So many people are ready to say, "Well, the Bible is wrong, because look..." No, the Bible isn't wrong. The interpretation is at fault.

I have encountered many people with faulty interpretations of scripture. If your interpretation of a scripture would cause it to seem ridiculous or foolish, then your interpretation of that scripture is wrong. God didn't say anything that was ridiculous or foolish. Rather than pointing the accusing finger at Scripture, it is more helpful to identify the basic problem with my limited understanding. It is far more productive to confess that the meaning of a passage eludes us than to throw up our hands and cry out, "Hopeless contradiction!" We must make every effort to understand what God is saying. We can be assured that when we discover the proper interpretation of a verse, it will be reasonable and rational and will not contradict the rest of the Scriptures.

It is crucial to remember that many of our problems with Scripture are a result of our own personal assumptions and biases. Many passages that can have a dual interpretation based on one's point of view. We may be looking at it in too limited a fashion, rather than considering the verse in its context. When a person comes up to me with a question about a passage, I immediately read the context. Most generally, I catch in its context the correct interpretation and show them that it reads in an entirely different way than what they were thinking.

"He That Believes in Me..."

Jesus declared that in the last days, those who don't believe in Him and do not believe His words will have to stand before God to be judged. He said He's not going to judge them. He didn't come to judge the world. He came to save the world. This brings to mind His conversation with the religious leader Nicodemus. Jesus told him, "God did not send his Son into the world to condemn the world, but that the world, through him might be saved. He that believeth on Him is not condemned." He reiterates the same point here, "I didn't come to judge the world, I came to save it." He affirms His mission was that of saving the world. He said in another passage, "I've come to seek and save that which was lost." To believe on him is to have everlasting life. It is to be saved from the penalty and the consequence of sin. It is to be saved from the judgment and the wrath of God that is to come against all the unrighteousness of men, even those who have held the truth of God in unrighteousness. "He that believeth on Me," Jesus said, "is not condemned." Paul the apostle said, "There is therefore now no condemnation to those that are in Jesus Christ..." It is important to note that Paul did say to the church, "We must all stand before the judgment seat of Christ." The kind of judgment Paul speaks of is one of rewards for the things we have done while we are in these bodies. It is like the judge's seat at the Olympics, where the various participants come up to receive medals for the victories they have won in a particular event. We will stand before Christ to receive our rewards.

For those who don't believe in Jesus, it is a different story. They will stand before the judgment seat of God to receive sentencing for their failure to believe the words of Jesus, and for their failure to receive the forgiveness that God offered them through Christ. I am certain that God will give each person a chance to plead their case. But I'm sure at that time every excuse that people might seek to offer will sound so totally ludicrous, most will be unable to even say a word.

So we have seen the claims of Jesus Christ, radical, spectacular, and glorious. He has claimed that he has come to save you. He has claimed that you can have eternal life through believing his words and following his commandments.

"Vanity, Vanity..."

The longer I live and the more I see of what the world has to offer, the more vain it seems. I see the emptiness that people experience who seem to have attained more worldly goods than the rest of us. In light of the hopelessness of even the best of this world, Jesus' offer of life is too good to turn down. I have no intellectual problems with this whatsoever. In fact, I would have great intellectual difficulties in not believing Jesus Christ because, I would have to rationalize his miracles. I would have to come up with an explanation for his ability to walk on the water, to raise Lazarus from the dead, and his own resurrection. I'd have to explain how one Man could, by accident, fulfill all 300 of the Messianic prophecies. I would find myself very hard pressed to try to give some kind of an explanation that would be rational or plausible.

"Choose You This Day Whom You Will Serve.."

Many years ago, I, like most people, experienced a time of doubt. I thought, "Well maybe I'm an atheist. Maybe God doesn't exist. Maybe it is all just the figment of man's imagination. Man needs something to believe in, so he invented a god, and the Bible is simply a collection of stories expressing man's concepts and ideas of a supreme being." That lasted for around a half hour until I started to critically evaluate this point of view. The moment I started thinking, and tried to explain the existence of universe apart from God, I had to yield to reason. To hold on to an explanation of life apart from God would require a mindless state akin to idiocy. I couldn't put myself in that kind of unreasonable state of mind. I would have to believe all kinds of absurdities. I would have to believe that such patently miraculous features of life, such as the marvelous ability to see, were created by thousands of fortuitous accidental circumstances. I would have to buy the idea that the perfect structure and function of the eye began with the sun beating down on a little worm and creating a mutation on its forehead. (I don't know how a worm would know what was his forehead and what was not.) But gradually over a process of time, through billions of years and countless mutations, this aberration formed into an eye and living things gained the ability to see. This same little worm scraped its tissue so often that it formed scar tissue which became legs complete with fully developed feet. Now our worm is a salamander and can see and walk. Is that rational? Give me a break!

"The fool has said in his heart there is no God." A person must take a very mindless position to try to argue away the evidence of design in creation. In my own experience, I found it was easier to believe in God than to deny his existence. Not to believe in God brought forth too many difficulties. I believe in the existence of God, which, according to scripture proves I'm not a fool. But every man has to make the choice to believe or not to believe. Jesus has made the claim that if you've seen him, you've seen the One who has sent him. If you believe on him, you believe on the One who has sent him. He claims that he came to save, that his words are eternal life and that they are not his words, but the words of the Father. The Father is the One who told him what to speak to us. If you don't believe, you're abiding in darkness and one day you will stand before God at the great judgment. I want to believe! I do believe! I have no problem with my belief.

God has provided such an abundance of evidence that any thinking, rational man can be completely satisfied in having faith in Jesus Christ. We can easily believe that he is the Son of God who came to save the world from sin. He came as light into this darkness, and those who hear his words and follow him do not walk in darkness but have the light of life. There are many infallible proofs that confirm the claims of Jesus. We pray for those who have been wrestling with this issue that they will come to a solid, strong faith in the Messiah of Israel, the Son of God, Immanuel, the Mighty God, Jesus of Nazareth.

APPENDIX I

THE MISHNAH, TALMUD & TARGUMS

Mishnah

Mishnah: Literally "repeated study," the Mishnah is the oldest post biblical collection and codification of the Jewish Oral Laws, systematically compiled by numerous authors over a period of two centuries. The Mishnah was completed around 200 C.E. by Rabbi Judah and represents various oral traditions that had been preserved since the time of Ezra, 450 B.C.E. It is made up of six Orders, called Sedarim and 63 tractates.

Talmud

The word Talmud means "study or learning" and is a commentary on the Mishnah. The Talmud contains quotes from the Mishnah with commentary called Gemara. When the Mishnah was combined with these commentaries, they were given the name Talmud.

The Talmud Bavi (Babylonian Talmud) was written from the years 200 - 400 C.E. and was taken from oral and written materials from the time of Ezra. It comments on the whole Mishnah while the Talmud Yerushalemi (Palestinian or Jerusalem Talmud), on which work ended in 500 C.E., comments mainly on the first four orders of the Mishnah. Authorities agree that it was never completed.

In 1631 the Talmud was edited to remove many of the references to Jesus of Nazareth because there were many

237

derogatory references to Jesus and the Church used these to justify persecution of the Jews.

Midrash

These are running commentaries on the Tanakh which date from as early as 100-200 C.E. and as late as 1600 C.E. The Midrash is divided as follows:

Halakah Midrashim comment mainly on the books Exodus, Leviticus, Numbers and Deuteronomy.

Mekhilta
Mekhlita deRabbi Shim'on ben Yohai
Sifra, Sifre, Sifre zuta.
Haggadah Midrashim expounds on the non-legal parts of scripture.
Midrash rabba 5th Century
Tanhuma 4th Century
Pesiqta de Rabbi Kahana
Pesiqta rabbati
Avat de Rabbi Natan
Tanna deve Eliyyahu
Pirqe de Rabbi Eliezer
Yakult Shimoni 13th century
Yakult ha-makhiri 14th century
Yakult 'En Ya'aqov 16th century

Targums

These are perhaps the oldest known commentaries on the Tanakh. The Targums are Aramaic translations of the original Hebrew Tanakh with the addition of rabbinical commentary on the text just translated. They were written between about 200 B.C.E.-200 C.E. The oldest extant manuscripts of Targum material is the Targum Onkelos from the third century C.E.

APPENDIX II

HISTORICAL EVIDENCE FOR JESUS OF NAZARETH

As a first year college student, at the age of eighteen, I was told by a Jewish friend of mine that Jesus of Nazareth was a non–historical figure, a hoax, contrived by a group of crafty co-conspirators in the first or second century. This effort to explain away the historical existence of Jesus of Nazareth has actually been seriously promoted by scholars for centuries. In fact, this is a common answer given in modern Jewish homes when a child asks "Who was Jesus?"

For years this explanation for the Jesus question seemed reasonable. However, my comfort level was eventually disturbed by some nagging questions.

Why would the Roman government brutally persecute peaceful followers of a non–historical figure? Why were tens of thousands of first century Christians (almost exclusively Jewish believers in Jesus), who lived within forty years of the "mythical events," willingly suffer the loss of all possessions and status, and be murdered for a myth? Why would Saul of Tarsus, a Jewish Pharisee, a leader of the Jews, be willing to give up everything and join the crowd that he had admittedly been persecuting? These are some of the questions that the myth theory doesn't satisfactorily explain.

Obviously, if Jesus of Nazareth was a true historical figure, and if he truly was who his disciples claimed he was, then there should be historical references to his existence other than the New Testament documents.

As we search for "extra biblical" (i.e. non-Christian) sources for the existence of Jesus, we will discover that the skeptic hasn't a leg to stand on when he argues that Jesus was a non–historical figure.[1] There are numerous historical references to Jesus, from both neutral and antagonistic sources, as early as the mid first century.

Secular Historical References to Jesus of Nazareth

When a historian sets out to prove the historical existence of an individual he seks out a number of sources. Perhaps the most reliable sources of historical evidence are from those who were not sympathetic to the person or his cause. A source that is either indifferent or antagonistic to Jesus or the church could not be accused of bias and, therefore, part of the "evil plot" to create a mythical figure. As we look at historical references we will try to focus mainly on such historic sources.

Flavius Josephus

Joseph ben Matthias was born in the year 37 C.E. and died around 100 C.E. As the son of a Jewish priest, he eventually became a priest himself and a member of the Pharisee sect of Judaism. In 64 C.E. he went to Rome to secure the release of certain priests and became convinced that Rome could not be defeated by the Jewish revolt which

---

[1] By extra–biblical sources, I mean references to the historical Jesus in writings other than the Bible.

began in 66 C.E. and ended in 70 C.E. when Jerusalem was sacked by the Romans.

In July 67 C.E., he was captured by Rome and was eventually hired as a scribe and an interpreter by the Roman government. At that time he was given the name Flavius Josephus by his Roman associates and wrote under that name.

In 70 C.E., he rode into Jerusalem with the Roman General Titus and observed the annihilation of Jerusalem. Josephus recorded incredibly graphic details about the destruction of Jerusalem, as well as the crucifixion and death of millions of Jews.

There are three passages in his writings that are pertinent to Christianity. In his, *Antiquities of the Jews,* book eighteen, chapter three, paragraph three, he makes a comment about Jesus of Nazareth.

> "Now, there was about this time, Jesus, a wise man, if it be lawful to call him a man, for he was a doer of wonderful works-a teacher of such men as received the truth with pleasure. He drew over to him both many of the Jews and many of the gentiles. He was [the] Christ; and when Pilate, at the suggestion of the principal men amongst us, had condemned him to the cross, those that loved him at the first did not forsake him, for he appeared to them alive again the third day, as the divine prophets had foretold these and ten thousand other wonderful things concerning him; and the tribe of Christians, so named from him, are not extinct at this day." [1]

Josephus verifies that Jesus was a historical figure who was crucified by Pontius Pilate, that he had a great

---

[1] *The Complete Works of Josephus,* Translated by William Whiston, Kregel Publications, Grand Rapids, Mich 49501.

following, did miracles and rose from the dead on the third day. He does not attempt to explain away the historicity of Jesus of Nazareth nor does he try to explain away the miracles or his resurrection from the dead. Consequently, this is an incredibly valuable historical reference to Jesus of Nazareth.

Needless to say, because of its testimony of Jesus, this passage, commonly called the *Testimonium Flavianum,* a very controversial passage. Critics have claimed that it was a Christian insertion. However, there is strong evidence from the ancient manuscripts that this passage was in the original.[1] It is present in all of the extant ancient manuscripts and was quoted by early church fathers, such as Eusebius, as early as 325 C.E.

The main points of contention are the statements, "He was the Messiah," "if it be lawful to call him a man," and "He appeared to them alive again the third day." Josephus, described as an Orthodox Jew by some scholars, was apparently never converted to Christianity. Origen, a third century Christian, states twice that Josephus "did not believe in Jesus as the Christ."[2] Therefore, opponents argue that it is very unlikely that he would ever say these things of Jesus. Most historians do, however, believe that the references to Jesus of Nazareth being "a wise man," "a doer of wonderful works," and being crucified under Pontius Pilate, are valid portions of Josephus' original work.

---

[1] For detailed discussion of the debate on the authenticity of this passage see *He Walked Among Us,* Josh McDowell, Bill Wilson, Here's Life Publishers, pg. 37.

[2] Origen, Against Celsus 1.47 and his Commentary on Matthew 10.17, in The Ante Nicene Fathers, Roberts, Alexander and Donaldson, James, editors. Wm. Eerdmans Publishing Co.,1973 American Reprint of Edinburg edition, Grand Rapids ,MI.

A complete fourth century Arabic version of Josephus' *Antiquities of the Jews*, which contains the *Testimonium*, includes basically the same content as the above text, with a couple of very slight variations. Instead of saying "He was the Christ," it says "He was so-called the Christ."

> "At this time there was a wise man who was called Jesus. And his conduct was good, and he was known to be virtuous. And many people from among the Jews and other nations became his disciples. Pilate condemned him to be crucified and to die. And those who had become his disciples did not abandon his discipleship. They reported that he had appeared to them three days after his crucifixion and that he was alive; accordingly, he was perhaps the Messiah concerning whom the prophets have recounted wonders."[1]

This very ancient copy of *Antiquities* increases significantly the reliability that Josephus did, in fact, make historical reference to Jesus of Nazareth. Although there are significant stylistic differences in this Arabic version, the basic elements of the Greek version are preserved in this text. Jesus is described as a historical figure who was crucified under Pontius Pilate. Regarding the Messiahship of Jesus, he is described in more neutral terms, stating, "He was perhaps the Messiah." Finally, this version confirms that Jesus was of excellent character, that he gathered many disciples to himself and that Christians were still in existence at that time.

This version can hardly be criticized as a Christian fabrication. It is very unlikely that a Christian in the second or third century would describe Jesus as "perhaps the Messiah." Christians at that time were routinely tortured

---

[1]Pines, Shlomo. *An Arabic Version of the Testamonium Flavianum and its Implications,* Jerusalem Academic Press, 1971.

and murdered for believing in Jesus; therefore, it is very unlikely that a person under such a threat would describe Jesus in such equivocal terms.

The next passage is also in *Antiquities of the Jews*, book eighteen, chapter five, paragraph two. Josephus states:

> "Now some of the Jews thought that the destruction of Herod's army came from God, and that very justly, as a punishment of what he did against **John, that was called the Baptist; for Herod slew him, who was a good man, and commanded the Jews to exercise virtue,** both as to righteousness towards one another, and piety towards God, and **so to come to baptism**; for that the washing [with water] would be acceptable to him, if they made use of it, not in order to the putting away, [or the remission] of some sins [only,] but for the purification of the body; supposing still that the soul was thoroughly purified beforehand by righteousness. Now, when many others came to crowd about him, for they were greatly moved by hearing his words, Herod, who feared lest the great influence of John had over the people might put it into his power and inclination to raise a rebellion, (for they seemed ready to do anything he should advise,) thought it best, by putting him to death, to prevent any mischief he might cause, and not to bring himself into difficulties, by sparing a man who might make him repent of it when it should be too late."

Although Jesus is not specifically mentioned in this passage, the portrayal of his forerunner, John the Baptist, is in complete agreement with the record of John in the New Testament. Therefore, the historical reliability of the New Testament overall is further established. To Josephus, John the Baptist was a historical figure. Josephus validates what the Christian New Testament says about John. He was a righteous man who had great popularity among the people and he baptized people for the remission of sins.

Almost all historians believe that this is a passage from the original text. It is also in the Arabic version.

The third reference is in *Antiquities of the Jews,* book twenty, chapter nine, paragraph one. This is in reference to the Jewish high priest, Ananius, and the brother of Jesus.

> "After the death of the procurator Festus, when Albinus was about to succeed him, the high-priest Ananius considered it a favorable opportunity to assemble the Sanhedrin. He therefore caused James the brother of Jesus, who was called Christ, and several others, to appear before this hastily assembled council, and pronounced upon them the sentence of death by stoning. All the wise men and strict observers of the law who were at Jerusalem expressed their disapprobation of this act...Some even went to Albinus himself, who had departed to Alexandria, to bring this breach of the law under his observation, and to inform him that Ananius had acted illegally in assembling the Sanhedrin without the Roman authority." (*Antiquities* 20:9)

Most historians believe that this passage was penned by Josephus and was not a Christian insertion. Louis Feldman, professor of Classics at Yeshiva University states:

> "Few have doubted the genuineness of this passage." [1]

These three references, though not without controversy, are considered by the majority of historians to be substantially from the pen of Josephus. Professor Shlomo Pines, a well known Israeli scholar, discusses the fact of Jesus' historicity and the references to Jesus by Josephus:

---

[1]Josephus, *Antiquities*, Leob Edition, vol IX, p. 496.

"In fact, as far as probabilities go, no believing Christian could have produced such a neutral text: for him the only significant point about it could have been its attesting the historical evidence of Jesus. But the fact is that until modern times this particular hare (i.e. claiming Jesus is a hoax) was never started. **Even the most bitter opponents of Christianity never expressed any doubt as to Jesus having really lived.**"[1]

Thallus

Thallus was an historian who lived in the middle of the first century C.E. His writings focus partly on the historical events of the Roman Empire of that Century. We do not have his original works, written around 52 C.E., but we do have the writings of men who referred to his work.

Julius Africanus, an early church father writing in the year 221 C.E., wrote about the writings of Thallus. In a document written by him, there is a discussion about the darkness that was recorded by the writers of the New Testament at the time of the crucifixion of Jesus.

"Now from the sixth hour until the ninth hour there was darkness over all the land."[2] (Matthew 27:45)

Now the skeptic might easily dismiss this event, recorded in the gospel of Matthew, as mere dramatics, an attempt to dress up the crucifixion event with some supernatural imagery. However, the darkness which occurred at the time of a full moon was recorded by Thallus.

---

[1]Pines, Shlomo, *An Arabic Version of the Testamonium Flavianum and its Implications*, Jerusalem Academic Press, 1971. pg 69
[2]That is, from noon to 3:00 pm.

Africanus notes that Thallus had attempted to explain away the event:

"Thallus, in the third book of his history explains away the darkness as an eclipse of the sun, unreasonably as it seems to me." [1]

Africanus, writing in the year 221 C.E., had access to the writings of Thallus. Thallus in his third book wrote that this darkness, which occurred during the reign of Caesar Tiberius, was a result of an eclipse of the sun. Africanus makes the point that this could not have been a solar eclipse, because the crucifixion took place at Passover which always occurs during a full moon and during a full moon, there can be no solar eclipse. Africanus recognized this.

An interesting aspect of this reference is that Thallus does not try to deny the existence of Jesus of Nazareth, the occurrence of his crucifixion nor the historical fact that the darkness occurred. He presents Jesus of Nazareth as a historical person, and the darkness as a historical event. His motive in writing about the darkness is to explain it as a natural event.

Philopon

Philopon, a sixth-century secular historian, wrote regarding Phlegon as well.[2] He wrote:

---

[1] Africanus, Chronography, 18:1, Roberts, Alexander and Donaldson, James, editors. *The Ante Nicene Fathers.* Wm Eerdmans Publishing Co.,1973 American Reprint of Edinburg edition, Grand Rapids ,MI.

[2] Africanus, Chronography, 18:1 in *The Ante Nicene Fathers,* Roberts, Alexander and Donaldson, James, editors. Wm. Eerdmans Publishing Co.,1973 American Reprint of Edinburg edition, Grand Rapids ,Mich.

"and about this darkness...Phlegon recalls it in his
book *The Olympiads.*"

Like Thallus, Phlegon verifies the historical existence of
Jesus of Nazareth and the historicity of the darkness which
occurred during the reign of Tiberius Caesar. These common
threads occurring in the writings of two men who were not
Christians is powerful evidence that Jesus is a historical
figure and an unnatural darkness (not an eclipse) occurred
during his life.

Tacitus

Cornelius Tacitus, born circa 52-55 C.E., became a
senator in the Roman government under Emperor
Vespasian. He was eventually promoted to governor of
Asia. Writing in the year 116 C.E. in his Annals, he writes
of the burning of Rome in 64 C.E. and how Caesar Nero had
tried to stop the rumor that he (Nero) was behind the
destruction.

"Therefore, to scotch the rumor (that Nero had
burned Rome) Nero substituted as culprits, and
punished with the utmost refinements of cruelty, a
class of men, loathed for their vices, whom the crowd
styled Christians. **Christus, the founder of the
name, had undergone the death penalty in the
reign of Tiberius, by sentence of the procurator
Pontius Pilatus**, and the pernicious superstition was
checked for a moment, only to break out once more,
not merely in Judea, the home of the disease, but in
the capital itself, where all things horrible or shameful
in the world collect and find a vogue.....**They [the
Christians] were covered with wild beasts' skins
and torn to death by dogs; or they were fastened
on crosses, and, when daylight failed were
burned to serve as lamps by night. Nero had
offered his Gardens for the spectacle, and gave**

an exhibition in his Circus, mixing with the crowd in the habit of a charioteer, or mounted on his car. Hence, in spite of a guilt which had earned the most exemplary punishment, there arose a sentiment of pity, due to the impression that they were being sacrificed not for the welfare of the state but to the ferocity of a single man." [1]

This amazing document verifies that Jesus, or Christus, was a true historical figure, that he lived and was killed during the reign of Caesar Tiberius, that he was sentenced under Pontius Pilate and that by about 64 C.E., Christianity had spread rapidly throughout the Roman empire. Tacitus verifies that Christians were viciously tortured by Nero only thirty-two years after the death of Jesus of Nazareth. The historical validity of this letter by Tacitus is doubted by very few scholars. According to some scholars, Tacitus is:

"Universally considered the most reliable of historians, a man in whom sensibility and imagination, though lively, could never spoil a critical sense rare in his time and a great honesty in the examination of the documents." [2]

Emperor Hadrian

During the period when Hadrian was emperor of Rome, 117-138 C.E., there continued to be tremendous persecution of Christians. Serenius Granianus, the governor of Asia at that time, wrote a letter to emperor Hadrian asking for his advice regarding how he should handle the Christians. Hadrian responded to Serenius' successor,

---

[1]Tacitus, Annals, Loeb edition 15.44.
[2]Amoit, Francois; Brunot, Amedee; Danielou, Jean; Daniel-Rops, Henri. *The Sources for the Life of Christ*. Translated by P.J. Herpburne-Scott. New York; Hawthorn Books, 1962, pg. 16.

Minucius Fundanus, and an excerpt from this letter, preserved by Eusebius follows:

> "I do not wish, therefore, that the matter should be passed by without examination, so that these men may neither be harassed, nor opportunity of malicious proceedings be offered to informers. If, therefore, the provincials can clearly evince their charges against the Christians, so as to answer before the tribunal, let them pursue this course only, but not by mere petitions, and mere outcries against the Christians. For it is far more proper, if anyone would bring an accusation, that you should examine it." [1]

This fascinating letter from the Roman emperor himself verifies the historical existence of the church, the belief that Christians were trouble-makers, that Christianity was illegal at that time and that Christians would be taken before a counselor simply for admitting that they were Christians. Though not a specific reference to Jesus of Nazareth, this very early historical reference to the church, its illegality in the Roman Empire and the persecutions (*malicious proceedings*) are powerful evidences for the rapid spread of the church within one generation of the life of Jesus. Therefore, this increases the reliability that Jesus was a historical figure and that the events surrounding his life were extraordinary, so much so that people were willing to die for the belief that he was the Messiah.

Lucian of Samosata

Lucan of Samosata, a Greek satirist, wrote a remarkable statement regarding the Church in 170 C.E.

---

[1] Eusebius, *The History of the Church*, 4.9.

"The Christians, you know, worship a man to this day–the distinguished personage who introduced their novel rites, and was crucified on that account...You see, these misguided creatures start with the general conviction that they are immortal for all time, which explains the contempt of death and voluntary self-devotion which are so common among them; and then it was impressed on them by their original lawgiver that they are all brothers, from the moment that they are converted, and deny the gods of Greece, and worship the crucified sage, and live after his laws. All this they take quite on faith, with the result that they despise all worldly goods alike, regarding them merely as common property." [1]

That is quite a testimony. This letter confirms that Christians worshipped a crucified Jewish sage, that they faced death bravely and that they despised worldly attributes. He explains this on the basis that Christians believed they were immortal and would spend eternity with God.

Mara Bar-Serapion

Mara Bar-Serapion, a Syrian and a stoic philosopher, wrote this letter to his son from prison sometime after 70 C.E.

"What advantage did the Athenians gain from putting Socrates to death? Famine and plague came upon them as a judgment for their crime. What advantage did the men of Samos gain from burning Pythagoras? In a moment their land was covered with sand. What advantage did the Jews gain from their executing their wise King? It was just after that that their kingdom was abolished. God justly avenged these three wise men: The Athenians died of hunger; the Samians were

---

[1]Lucian, The Death of Pregrine 11-13.

overwhelmed by the sea; the Jews, ruined and driven from their land, live in complete dispersion. But Socrates did not die for good; he lived on in the statue of Plato. Pythagoras did not die for good; he lived on in the statue of Hera. Nor did the wise King die for good; he lived on in the teaching which he had given."[1]

This letter refers to Jesus of Nazareth as being the "wise King." The writer is obviously not a Christian because he places Jesus on a par with Pythagoras and Socrates. Consequently, the writer can hardly be described as biased in his reference to Jesus and the church. Therefore, it is a valuable historical reference regarding the historicity of Jesus. There are many other non-Christian historical sources for Jesus of Nazareth but since space is limited we will move on to rabbinical sources.

Ancient Rabbinical References to Y'shua (Jesus)

Of all the ancient historical sources for Jesus of Nazareth, the least favorably biased would have to be rabbinic in origin. There are actually quite a large number of such references to Jesus of Nazareth. The problem with the rabbinical writings is that they use names like "such and such" and "so and so" or "that man" when they refer to Jesus of Nazareth. Consequently, some of the references are considered to be unreliable. During the middle ages and the early renaissance, the Talmud and Midrash were cleaned up with the removal of most of the references to Jesus of Nazareth.

As expected, the remaining references to Jesus are very unflattering. However, they do verify a number of important historical facts that the gospels proclaim

[1]British Museum Syriac MS. Addition 14, 658.

regarding Jesus of Nazareth. As mentioned earlier by Shlomo Pines, no one doubted that Jesus was an historical figure up until about 200-300 years ago. The myth theory was created and perpetuated by atheists and agnostics and embraced by mainstream Judaism during the Renaissance.

In the Babylonian Talmud, which was compiled between the years 200-500 C.E., in Sanhedrin 43a, there is a fascinating reference to Jesus of Nazareth:

> "It has been taught: On the Eve of the Passover, they hanged Yeshu. And an announcer went out in front of him, for forty days saying: 'he is going to be stoned because he practiced sorcery and enticed and led Israel astray. Anyone who knows anything in his favor, let him come and plead in his behalf.' But, not having found anything in his favor, they hanged him on the Eve of the Passover."

This is considered to be one of the very reliable rabbinical references to Jesus ("Yeshu"). The writer here verifies that Jesus of Nazareth was a historical figure, that he was crucified on the Eve of the Passover and that he did miracles, referred to as sorcery. The supernatural events surrounding the life of Jesus were not denied, but verified. The miracles of Jesus were simply explained away as being from a demonic source, i.e., sorcery.

According to Jewish law it is illegal to perform capital punishment on the Eve of the Passover. However, this record verifies something that we wouldn't expect to find in a rabbinical source, the fact that the Sanhedrin acted illegally in condemning and crucifying Jesus on Passover. Consequently, this reference is even more valuable in terms of validating the historicity of Jesus. Certainly, if any passage should have been edited from the Talmud, it should have been this one. The fact that a passage which points out an illegal action was retained in the Talmud makes it a credible and valuable source for the historicity of Jesus.

In the Talmud, Sanhedrin 43a, it says,

"Our Rabbis taught that Yeshu had five disciples: Matti, Necki, Netsur, Burni, and Toda."

Now one of those names we can recognize, Matti, the disciple named Matthew. Again it is considered by historians to be another reliable reference in the Talmud for the historicity of Jesus of Nazareth.

Maimonides

Maimonides was a very highly revered thirteenth century rabbi. There was a saying back during the thirteenth century that, "there was never a greater man than Maimonides except Moses." He was given the nickname, Rambam.

Maimonides wrote a fourteen volume work called the *Mishne Torah* in which he made multiple references to the historical existence of Jesus of Nazareth. However, in the year 1631, Catholic and Jewish authorities censored the fourteenth volume, removing all references to Jesus. This was done because of multiple derogatory references to Jesus of Nazareth. During the Spanish inquisition certain members of the Catholic church used Maimonides' work, and his negative references about Jesus, to justify the killing of Jews. Consequently, these references were removed from most of the extant volumes of Maimonides' writings.

An excerpt from the uncensored versions of the Mishne Torah is a remarkable historical reference to Jesus.[1]

"Jesus of Nazareth who aspired to be the Messiah and was executed by the court was also [alluded to] in Daniel's prophecies (Daniel 11:14), as 'the vulgar [common] among your people shall exalt themselves in an attempt to fulfill the vision, but they shall stumble.' **Can there be a greater stumbling block than Christianity?** All the prophets spoke of the Messiah as the Redeemer of Israel and its Savior, who would gather their dispersed and strengthen their [observation of] the Mitzvot [the commandments]. By contrast, [Christianity] caused the Jews to be slain by the sword, their remnant to be scattered and humbled, the Torah to be altered and the majority of the world to err and serve a god other than the Lord. Nevertheless, the intent of the Creator of the world is not within the power of man to comprehend, for his ways are not our ways, nor are his thoughts, our thoughts. [Ultimately,] all the deeds of Jesus of Nazareth and that Ishmaelite [Mohammed] who arose after him will only serve to prepare the way for the Messiah's coming and the improvement of the entire world [motivating the nations] to serve God together, as [Zephaniah 3:9] states: 'I will make the peoples pure of speech that they will all call upon the Name of God and serve him with one purpose.' "

Here Maimonides, writing in the thirteenth century, verifies that Jesus of Nazareth was executed by the Sanhedrin, that he aspired to be the Messiah, that he was referred to in the prophecies of Daniel as one of the sons of the lawless and that Jesus of Nazareth led many astray.

It is fascinating that Maimonides calls Jesus and his Church "a stumbling block." I don't think Maimonides

---

[1]*Heaven the Last Frontier*, Jeffrey, Grant; Frontier Research Publications.

remembered that the Tanakh states that the Messiah would be a stumbling block to both houses of Israel.

"He will be as a sanctuary, but a stone of stumbling and a rock of offense to both the houses of Israel, as a trap and a snare to the inhabitants of Jerusalem." (Isaiah 8:14)

Surely Jesus of Nazareth was a historical figure and his life, message, ministry was a stumbling block to the Jews of his day.

APPENDIX III

RABBINICAL QUOTES ON ISAIAH
52:13–53:12[1]

The purpose of this appendix is to present a number of rabbinical views on the fourth "suffering servant song," Isaiah 52:13–53:12. As you will see, there were differing opinions on this portion of scripture. However, the Messianic application of Isaiah 52-53 by the ancients was certainly a majority opinion.

Targum of Jonathan on Isaiah 52:13[2]

"Behold, my servant Messiah shall prosper; he shall be high and increase, and be exceedingly strong."

Targum of Jonathan on Isaiah 53:11-12[3]

"He [Messiah] shall save them from the servitude of the nations, they shall see the punishment of their enemies and be seated with the spoil of their kings. By his wisdom he shall vindicate the meritorious, in order to bring many to be subservient to the Torah, and he

---

[1]Portions in bold are actual paraphrases or quotes from Isaiah 52:13-53:12.
[2]The Targum of Yonathan Ben 'Uzziel,, Paris and Oxford Editions. See *The Fifty Third Chapter of Isaiah According to Jewish Interpreters,* preface pg. iv, S.R. Driver, A.D. Neubauer, KTAV Publishing House, Inc. ,New York ,1969
[3]ibid, preface pg. iv.

shall seek forgiveness for their sins. Then I will
apportion unto him the spoil of great nations, and he
shall divide the spoil the wealth of mighty cities,
because he was ready to suffer martyrdom that the
rebellious might subjugate to the Torah. And he shall
seek pardon for the sins of many, and for his sake the
rebellious shall be forgiven."

Babylonian Talmud folio 98b

"The Messiah—what is his name?...The Rabbis say,
'The leprous one, those of the house of Rabbi say,
'The sick one,' as it is said, '**Surely he hath borne
our sicknesses**,' etc.."[1]

Midrash Ruth Rabbah

"Another explanation [of Ruth 2:14]: He is speaking
of the King Messiah: 'Come hither,' draw near to the
throne; 'and eat of the bread,' that is, the bread of the
kingdom; 'and dip thy morsel in the vinegar,' this
refers to the chastisements, as it is said, '**But he was
wounded for our transgressions, bruised for our
iniquities.**'"[2]

Yalqut ii57I

"Who art thou, O great mountain? (Zechariah 4:7)
This refers to the King Messiah. And why does he call
him 'the great mountain?' Because he is greater than
the patriarchs, as it is said, '**My servant shall be
high, and lifted up, and lofty exceedingly**'; he

---

[1] Introduction to Jewish Literature, Etheridge, pg 409. For a detailed
discussion of this reference see *The Fifty Third Chapter of Isaiah
According to Jewish Interpreters,* preface, pg. iv, S.R. Driver, A.D.
Neubauer, KTAV Publishing House, Inc. ,New York, 1969
[2] ibid pg. 409

will be higher than Abraham, who says, 'I raise high
my hands unto the Lord' (Genesis 14:22); lifted up
above Moses, to whom it is said, 'Lift it up into thy
bosom' (Numbers 11:12); loftier than the ministering
angels, of whom it is written, 'Their wheels were lofty
and terrible' (Ezekiel 1:1). And out of whom does he
come forth? Out of David (Psalm 2:6). According to
another view this means, 'I have woven him,' cf.
Judges 16:14: i.e., I have drawn him out of the
chastisements. Rabbi Huna, on the authority of Rabbi
Aha, says, '**The chastisements are divided into
three parts: one for David and the fathers, one
for our own generation, and one for the King
Messiah; and this is that which is written, 'He
was wounded for our transgressions,' etc.**"[1]

Siphre [2]

"How much more, then, will the King Messiah, who
endures affliction and pains for the transgressors, as it
is written, 'He was wounded,' etc., justify all
generations! And this is what is meant when it is said,
'And the Lord made the iniquity of us all meet upon
him.' "

Thanhuma [3]

"Rabbi Nachman says, 'The word 'man' in the
passage, every man a head of the house of his fathers
(Num. 1:4), refers to the Messiah the son of David, as
it is written, 'Behold the man whose name is 'Zemah'
(the branch), where Yonathan interprets, 'Behold the

---

[1]Etheridge, pg. 409.
[2]See the monumental work Pugio Fidei, Martini, Raymundus, published by
De Vosin in 1651. For a detailed discussion of this reference see *The Fifty
Third Chapter of Isaiah According to Jewish Interpreters,* preface pg.iv
S.R. Driver, A.D. Neubauer, KTAV Publishing House, Inc. New York 1969
[3] Etheridge, pg. 409.

man Messiah (Zech. 6:12); and so it is said, '**a man of pains' and known to sickness.**' "

P'Siqtha (According to Hulsius)[1]

"The Holy One brought forth the soul of the Messiah, and said to him, 'Art thou willing to be created and to redeem my sons after 6000 years?' He replied, 'I am.' God replied, 'If so, thou must take upon thyself chastisements in order to wipe away their iniquity, as it is written, '**Surely our sicknesses he hath carried.**' The Messiah answered, 'I will take them upon me gladly.' "

Zohar, Section שיקהל

"There is in the garden of Eden a palace called the Palace of the sons of sickness: this palace the Messiah then enters and summons every sickness, every pain, and every chastisement of Israel; they come and rest upon him. And were it not that he had thus lightened them off Israel and taken them upon himself, there had been no man able to bear Israel's chastisements for transgression of the law: and this is that which is written, '**Surely our sicknesses he hath carried.**'"

Yepheth Ben 'Ali [2]

"Others of them think the subject of it (Isaiah 53) to be David and the Messiah, saying all the expressions of contempt, such as 'many were desolated at thee,' refer to the seed of David who are in exile; and all the

---

[1] 1Theologia Judaica, Hulsius pg. 328.

[2] The translation and commentary by the Quaraite (Jews who reject the traditions of the Talmud), Yepheth Ben 'Ali, a commentary of Sa'adyah's, according to the MS., No. 569, in the Imperial Library at St Petersburg.

glorious things, such as '**behold my servant will be prosperous**' and 'so shall he sprinkle,' refer to the Messiah. As to myself, I am inclined, with Benjamin of Nehawend, to regard it as alluding to the Messiah, and as opening with a description of his condition in exile, from the time of his birth to his accession to the throne: for the prophet begins by his being seated in a position of great honour, and then goes back to relate all that will happen to him during the captivity. He thus gives us to understand two things: In the first instance, that the Messiah will only reach his highest degree of honour after long and severe trials; and secondly, that these trials will be sent upon him as a kind of sign, so that, if he finds himself under the yoke of misfortunes whilst remaining pure in his actions, he may know that he is the desired one, as we shall explain in the course of this section. The expression '**my servant**' is applied to the Messiah as it is applied to his ancestor in the verse, 'I have sworn to David my servant' (Ps. 84:4)...By the words '**surely he hath carried our sicknesses**,' they mean that the pains and sicknesses which he fell into were merited by them, but that he bore them instead: the next words '**yet we did esteem him**,' etc., intimate that they thought him afflicted by God for his own sins, as they distinctly say, '**smitten of God and afflicted**.' And here I think it necessary to pause for a few moments, in order to explain why God caused these sicknesses to attach themselves to the Messiah for the sake of Israel...Inasmuch now as at the end of captivity there will be no prophet to intercede at the time of distress, the time of the Lord's anger and of his fury, God appoints his servant to carry their sins, and by doing so lighten their punishment in order that Israel might not be completely exterminated. Thus from the words 'he was wounded for our transgressions', we learn two things: 1) that Israel had committed many sins and transgressions, for which they deserved the indignation of God; 2) that by the Messiah bearing them they would be delivered from the wrath which rested upon them, and be able to endure it, as it is said, 'And by associating with him we are healed.' God will indeed afflict the Messiah with longer and severer sicknesses than Ezekiel."

Mysteries of Rabbi Shim'on Ben Yohai (Compiled in the Eleventh Century)[1]

"And Armilaus will join the battle with Messiah, the son of Ephraim, in the East gate...and Messiah, the son of Ephraim, will die there, and Israel will mourn for him. And afterwards the Holy One will reveal to them Messiah, the son of David, whom Israel will desire to stone, saying, Thou speakest falsely; already the Messiah is slain, and there is none other Messiah to stand up (after him): and so they will despise him, as it is written, '**Despised and forlorn of men**'; but he will turn and hide himself from them, according to the words, '**Like one hiding his face from us.**'" [2]

Rabbi Mosheh Ben Nachman (1250-1270 C.E.)[3]

"The right view respecting this Parashah is to suppose that by the phrase 'my servant' the whole of Israel is meant, as in Isaiah 44:2, and often. As a different opinion however is adopted by the Midrash, which refers it to the Messiah, it is necessary for us to explain it in conformity with the view there maintained. The prophet says, The Messiah, the son of David, of whom the text speaks, will never be conquered or perish by the hands of his enemies. And in fact, the text teaches this clearly.[4] In agreement with the words of Daniel, Isaiah says the Messiah, the

---

[1]Beth ham-Midrash, Jellinek, (1855) part ii, p.80.
[2]For a detailed discussion of this reference see *The Fifty Third Chapter of Isaiah According to Jewish Interpreters*, pg. 32, S.R. Driver, A.D. Neubauer, KTAV Publishing House, Inc. , New York, 1969.
[3]ibid, preface pg. ix , see # 20.
[4]That is, the text of Isaiah 53 clearly means that the Messiah will suffer and die at the hands of his enemies.

servant of the Lord, will understand: he will perceive the end, and forthwith will rise up and be exalted, and his heart will be 'lofty in the ways of the Lord' (2 Chronicles 17:6) to go and gather the outcasts of Israel, 'not by strength and not by might, but by his spirit' (Zechariah 4:6), trusting in the Lord, after the manner of that first redeemer who came with Pharaoh with his staff and scrip (cf. 1 Samuel 17:40), and smote his land with the 'rod of his mouth' (Isaiah 11:4). And so it is said in the Midrash, 'He will be higher than Abraham, more exalted than Moses, and loftier than the Ministering angels'; the Messiah, that is, will be higher than Abraham, who was an expounder of the belief in God and, in spite of the opposition of the king, gained proselytes in the land of Nimrod: for the Messiah will do more than he did; he will proselytize many nations. And he will be more exalted than Moses: Moses went in unto Pharaoh, the great and wicked king, who said, I know not the Lord (Exodus 5:2), and, although only a shepherd and the humblest of men, was not afraid of him, brought forth his people out of the 'furnace of iron' (Deuteronomy 4:20, Jeremiah 11:4). But the Messiah will do more than Moses: for he will stir himself up against the kings of the whole world, so as to bring forth Israel from their hands, and to execute vengeance upon the Gentiles. And he will be loftier than the ministering angels, for although they exert themselves diligently in the redemption of Israel (like Michael, Daniel 10:20,21), yet the Messiah will achieve more than the whole of them together. And wisdom will accompany this elevation of the Messiah, and his nearness to God: for neither Abraham, whom the glorious and fearful Name speak of as his friend (Isaiah 41:8), and with whom also he made a covenant; nor Moses, who was nearer to the Deity than any man; nor the ministering angels, who 'stand round about him on his right hand and on his left' (1 Kings 22:19), approach so closely to the knowledge of the Almighty as the Messiah; for of him it is written that he 'came to the Ancient of days', and that they 'brought him near before him' (Daniel 7:13), but of the angels it is only said that 'ten thousand times ten thousand stood before him...' The

text continues, referring still to *the Messiah,* '**A s
many were astonished by thee.**' Their
astonishment was shewn by mocking him when he
first arrived, and by asking how one 'despised', 'meek
and riding upon an ass' (Zechariah 9:9) could conquer
all those kings of the world who had laid hold of Israel,
and rescue him from their hand...For in the beginning
he was 'like a small tree' springing up '**out of the dry
earth,**' which never grows great enough to put forth
boughs and to bear fruit: he was '**despised,**' for he had
no army and no people, but was 'meek and riding upon
an ass,' like the first redeemer Moses, our master,
when he entered with his wife and children upon an ass
(Exodus 4:2)... '**He was oppressed and he was
afflicted**': for when he first comes,[1] 'meek and
riding upon an ass,' the oppressors and officers of
every city will come to him, and will afflict him with
revilings and with insults, reproaching both him and
the God in whose name he appears, like Moses our
master...The prophet continues: 'And because he was
numbered with the transgressor,' expected, as I have
stated, to be reckoned amongst them, 'and carried the
sin of many'– what happened to him at that time was
not for his own sins, but for the sins of others– 'and
for the transgressors,' i.e. (according to what is said
above, verse 6) 'allowed' the iniquity of sinners and
transgressors 'to light' upon himself."

Rabbi Mosheh Kohen Ibn Crispin [2]

"This Parashah the commentators agree in explaining
of the captivity of Israel, although the singular
number is used in it throughout. The expression 'my
servant' they compare rashly with Isaiah 41:8, 'thou

---

[1]Could it be that the rabbis here intimating that the Messiah will come
twice?
[2]A Commentary of Rabbi Mosheh Kohen Ibn Crispin of Cordova. For a
detailed discussion of this reference see The Fifty Third Chapter of Isaiah
According to Jewish Interpreters, preface pg. x, S.R. Driver, A.D. Neubauer,
KTAV Publishing House, Inc. New York 1969